I0391208

Next Level Mandala

coloring and inking for all

FIND YOUR OWN MEANING WITHIN THE MANDALA

William T Dixon

INTRODUCTION

I created Next Level Mandala for the colorist and the inkist. There appeared to be a need within the adult coloring book family to include those colorists that also enjoy inking and finding their own way, maybe even a little doodling too.

Next Level Mandala has been drawn with very fine lines, giving you the option of finding your own patterns within the design. You might also enjoy inking the pattern with different colors or just blending the colors between the mandala's sections.

Thank you for purchasing Next Level Mandala.

LET YOUR MIND'S EYE WANDER AND SEE YOUR OWN DESIGN WITHIN THE PATTERN

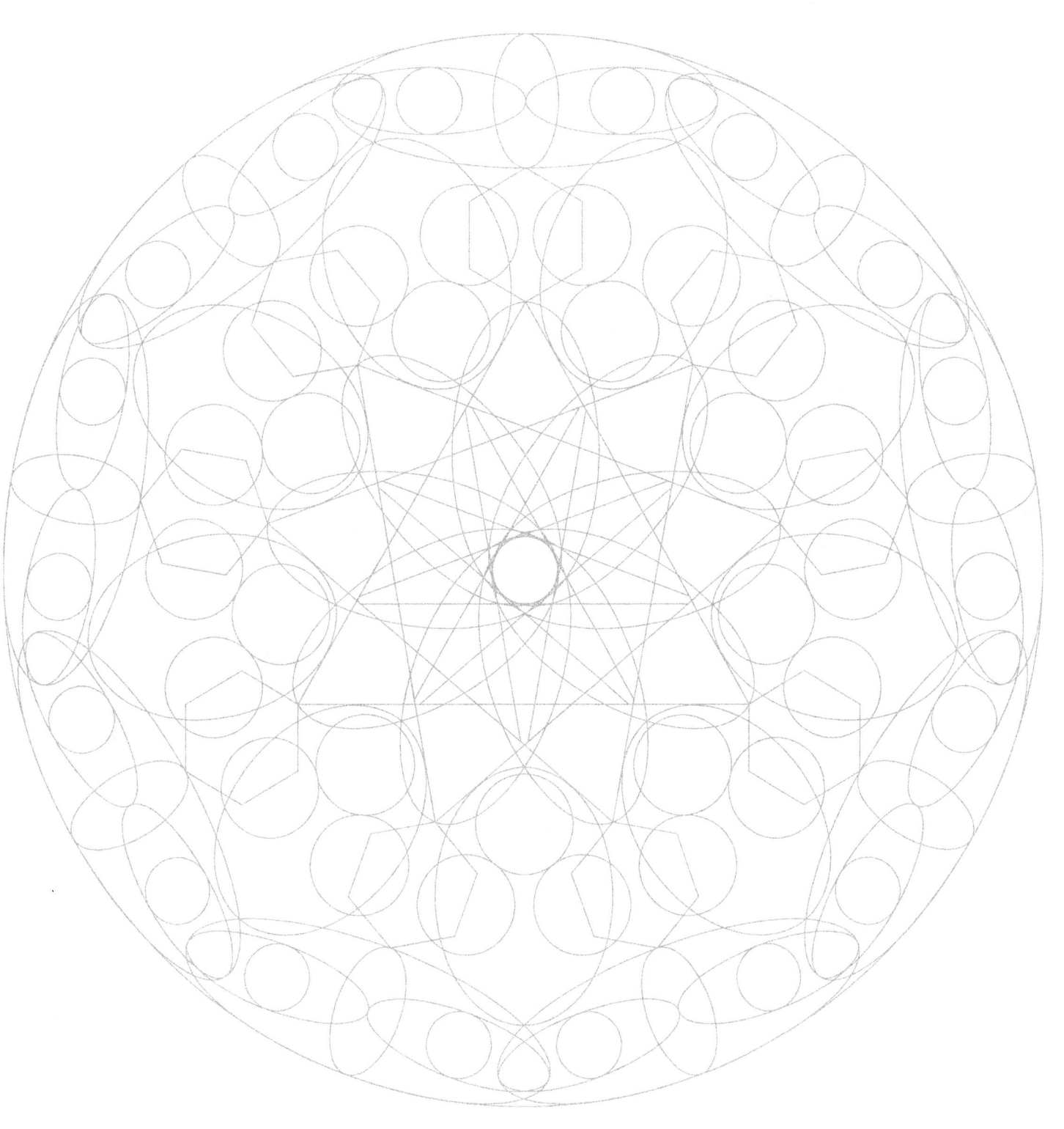

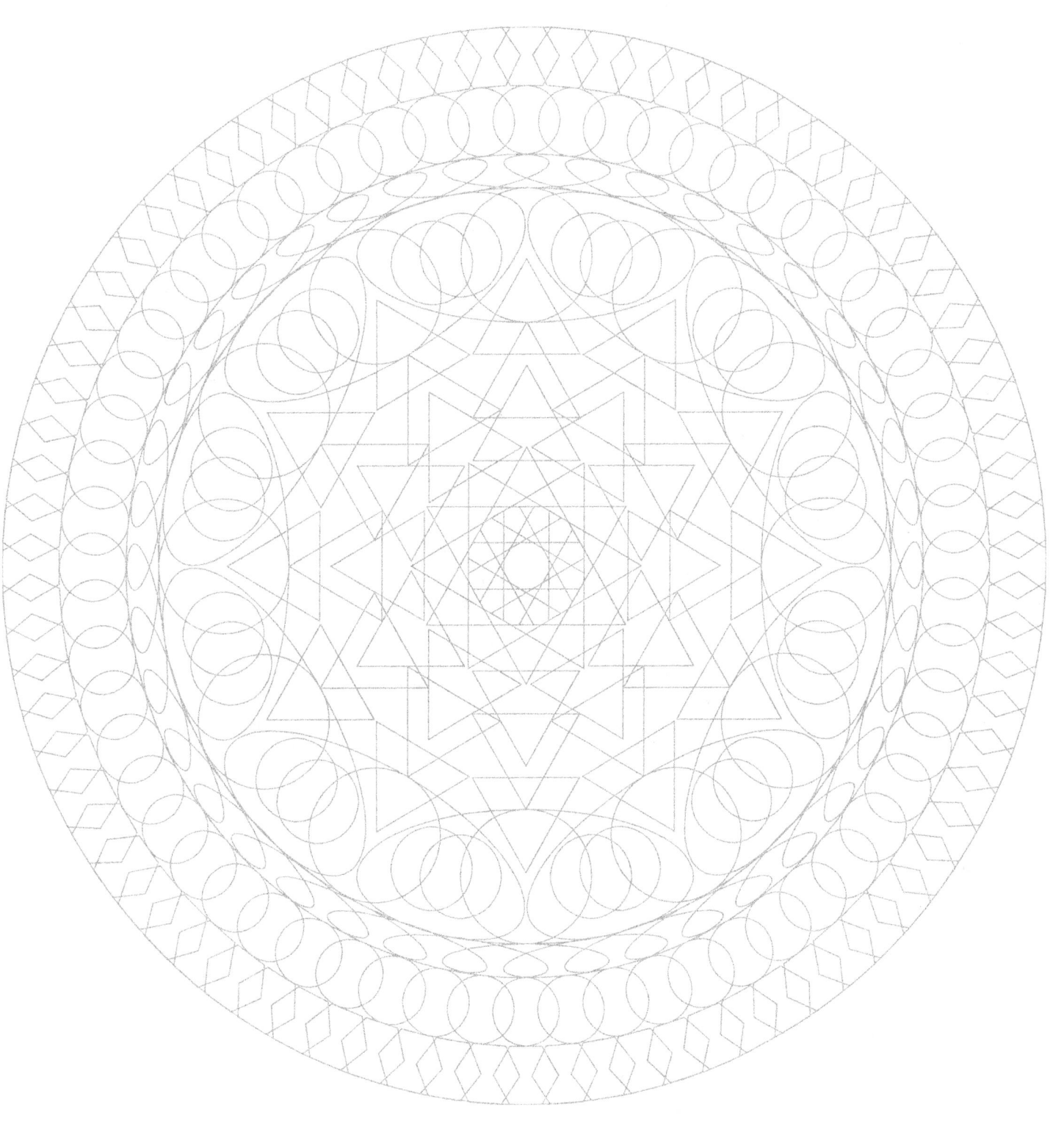

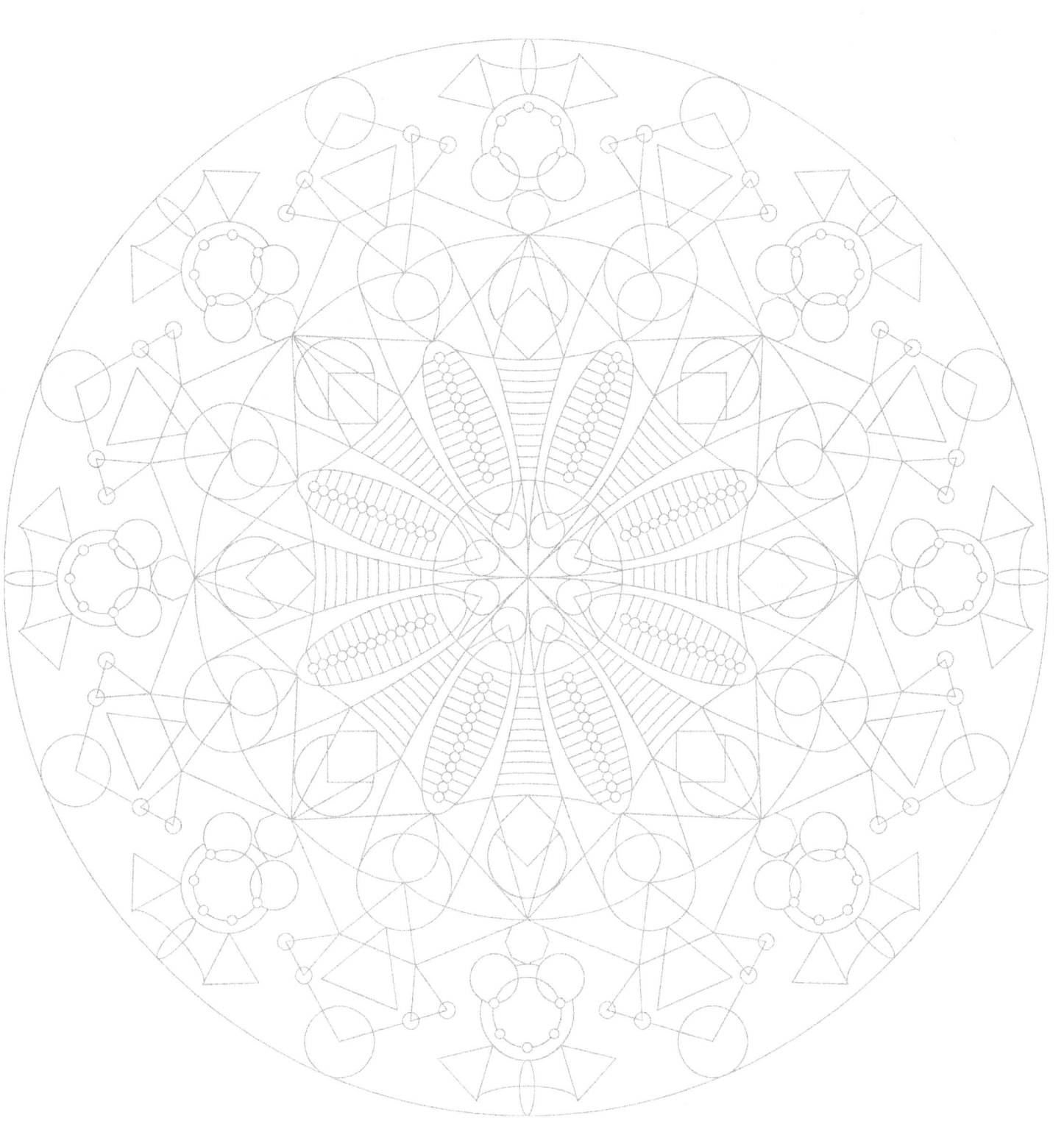

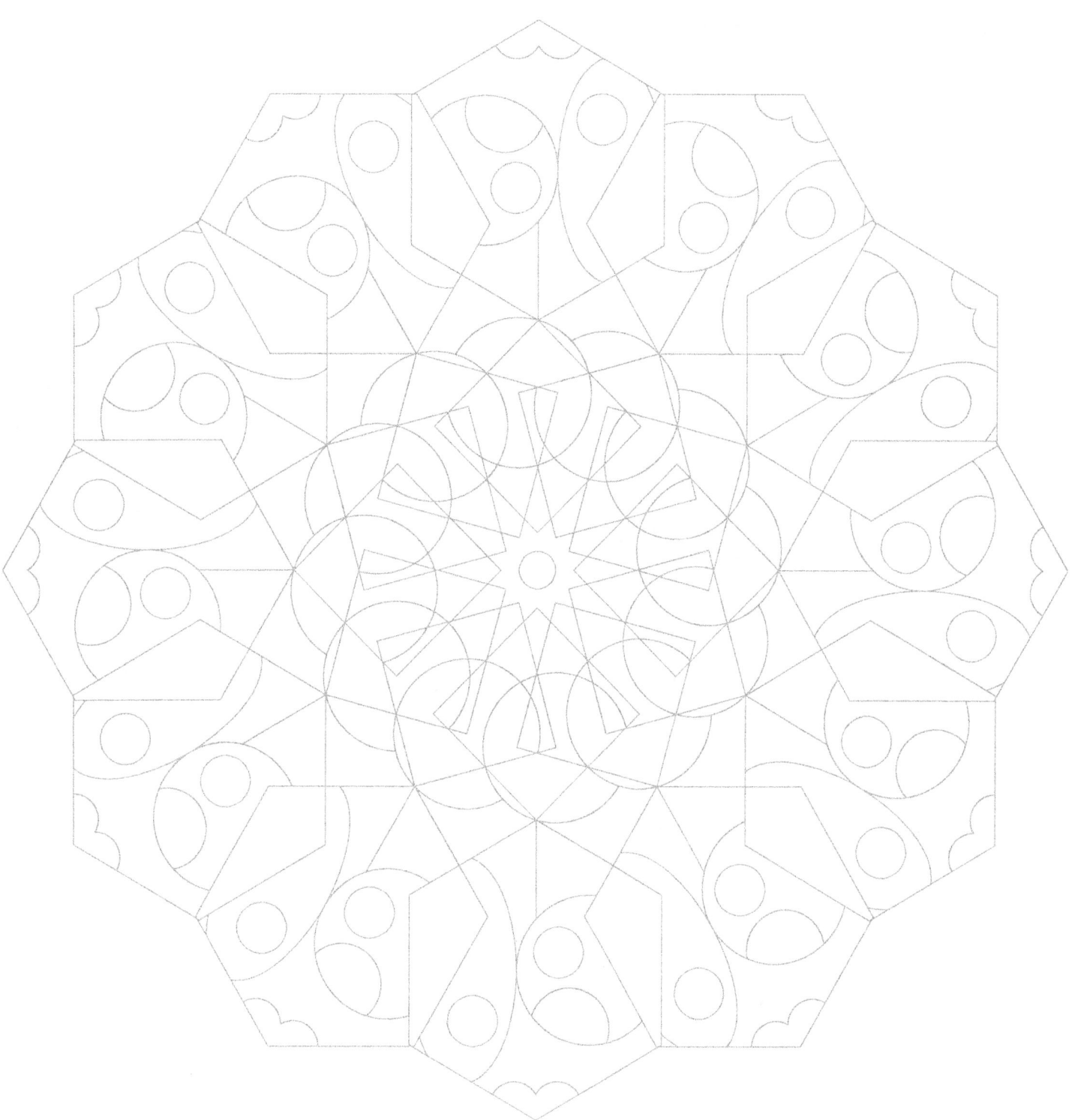

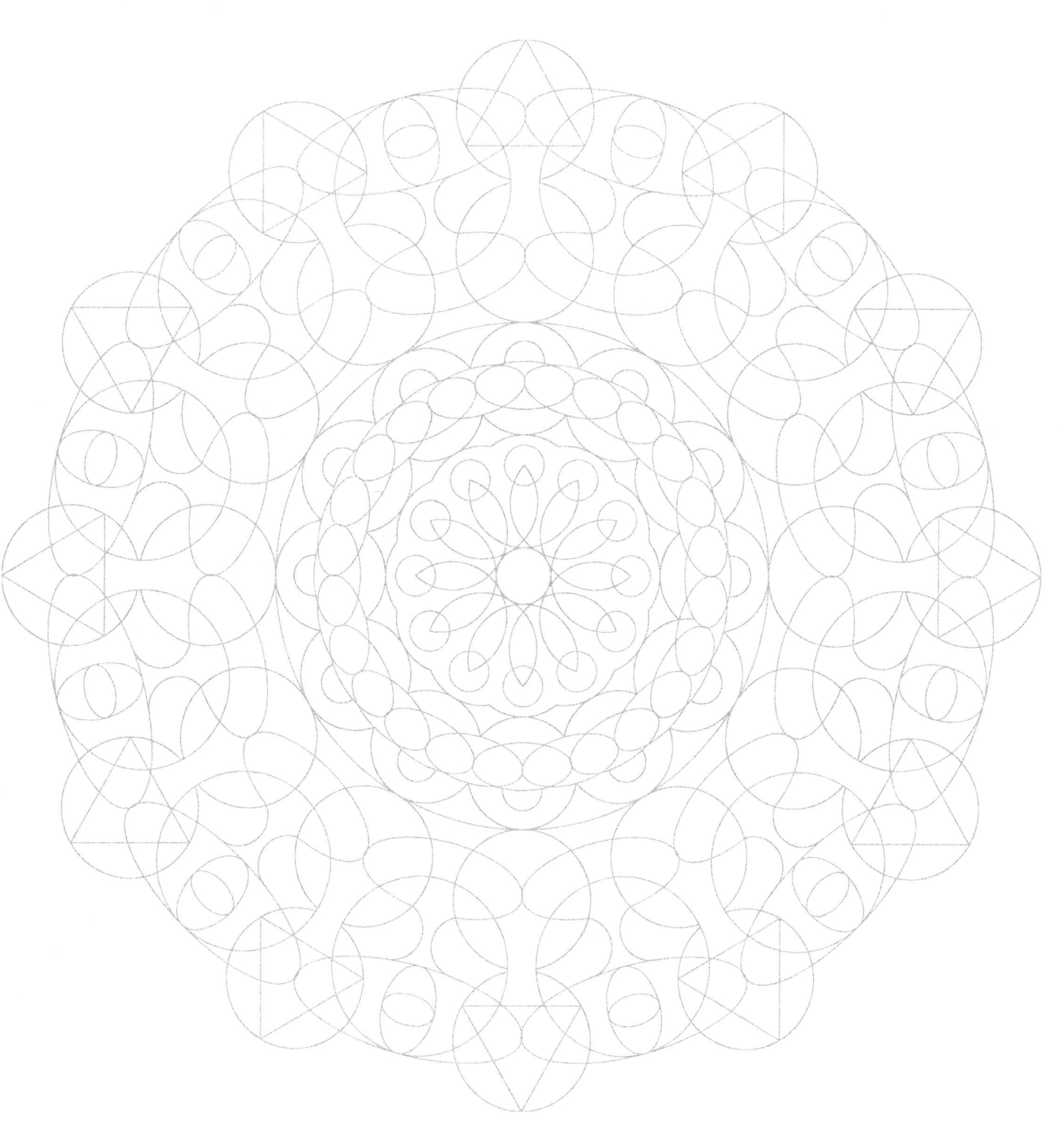

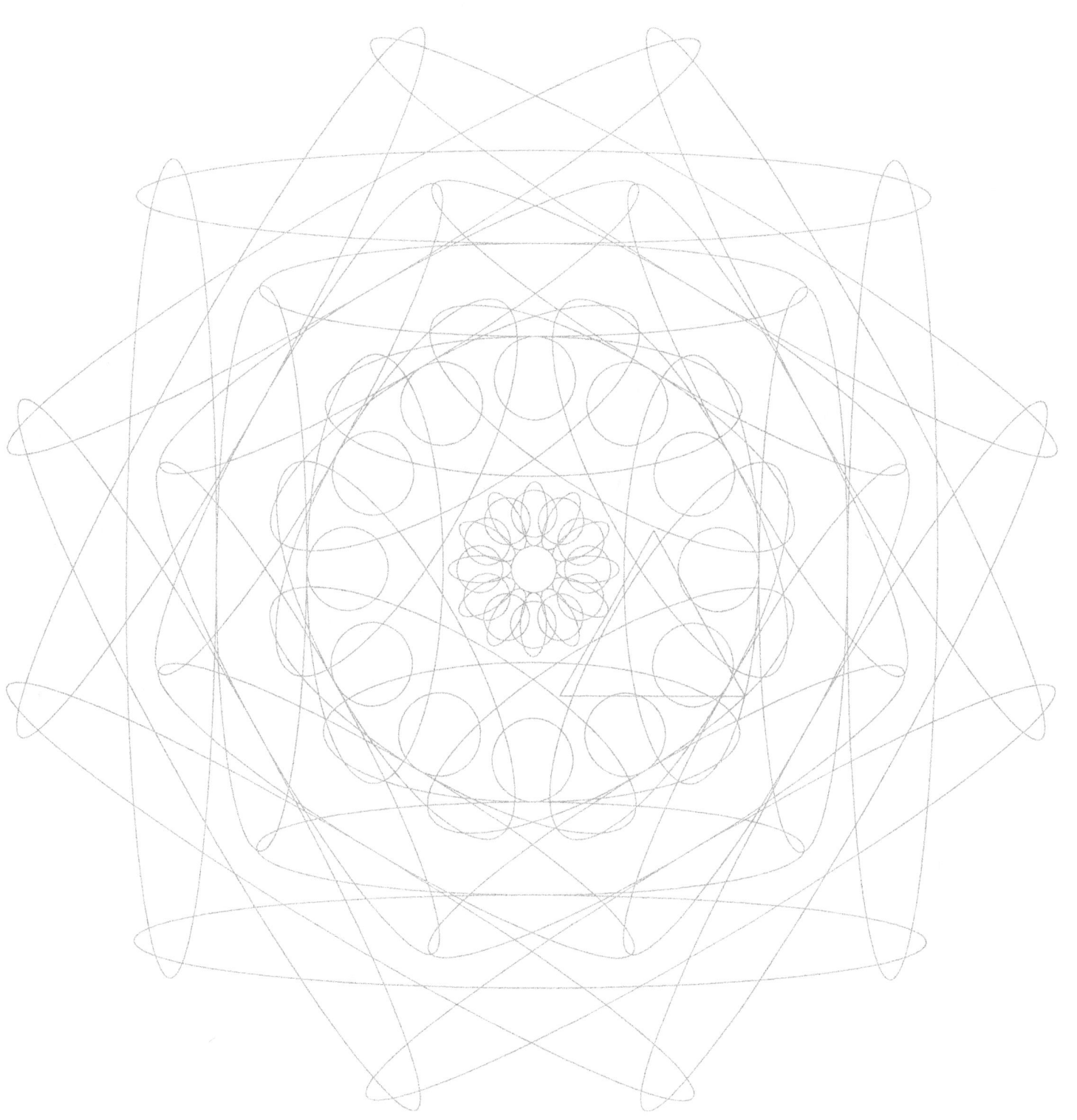

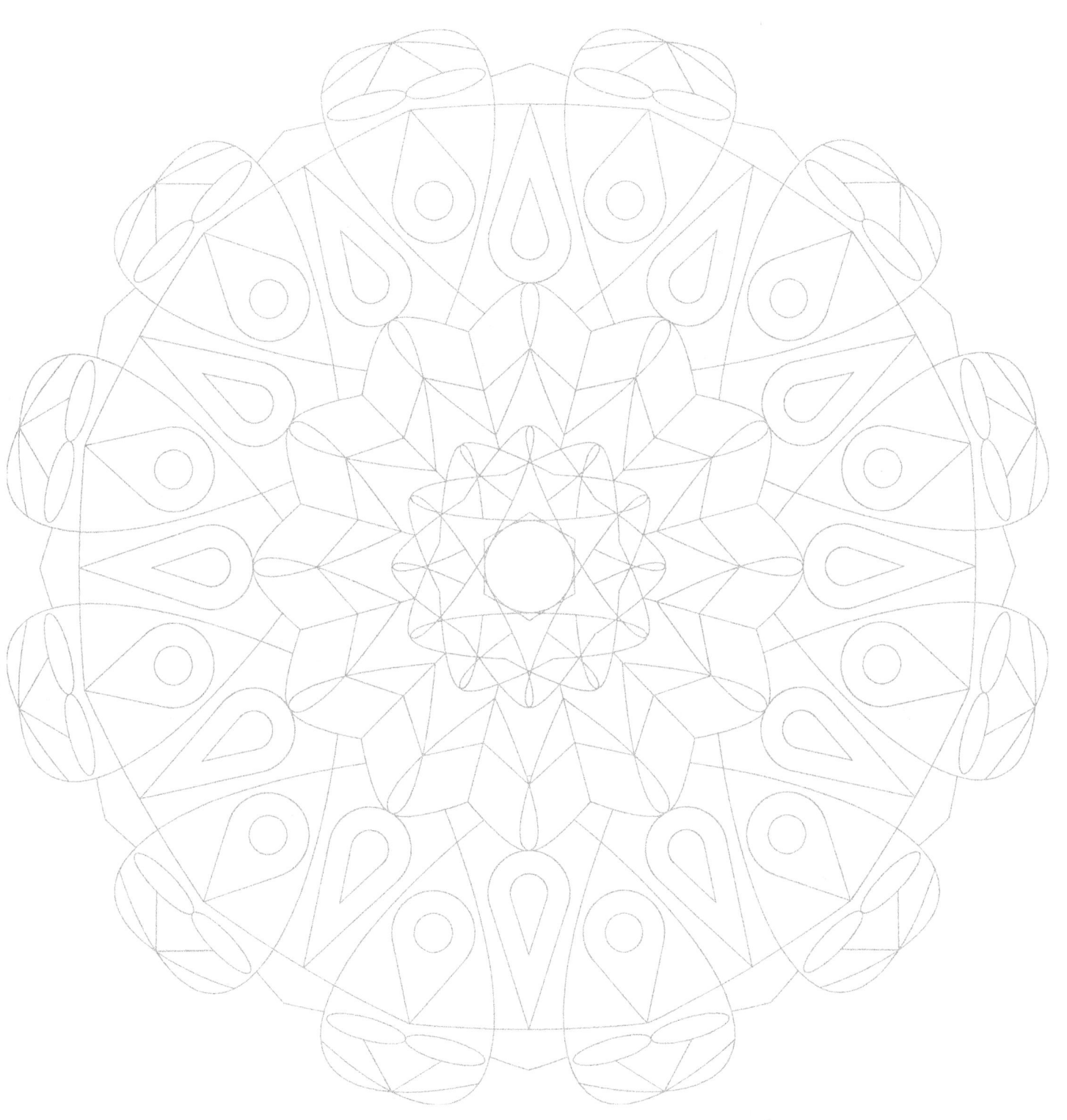

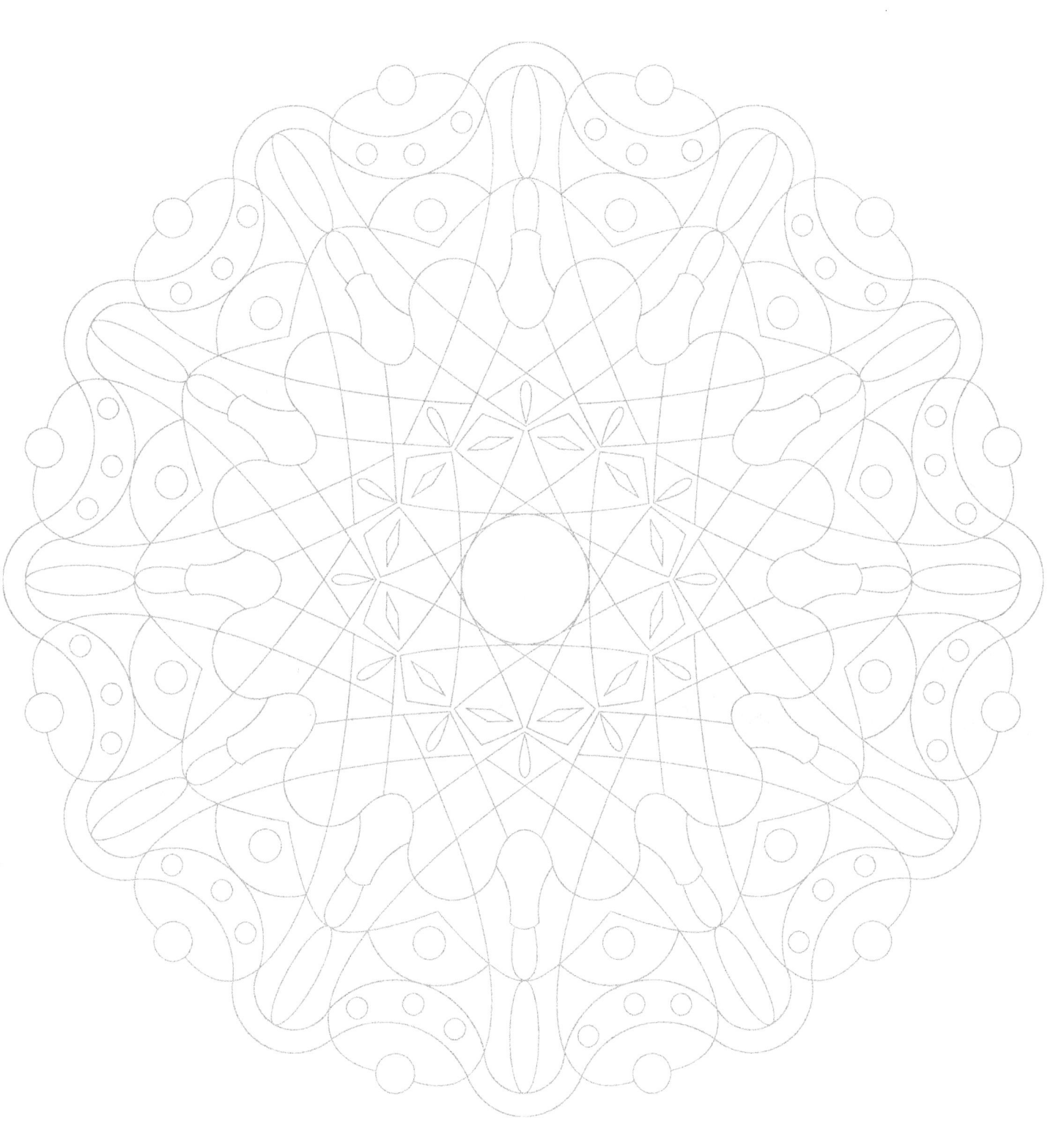

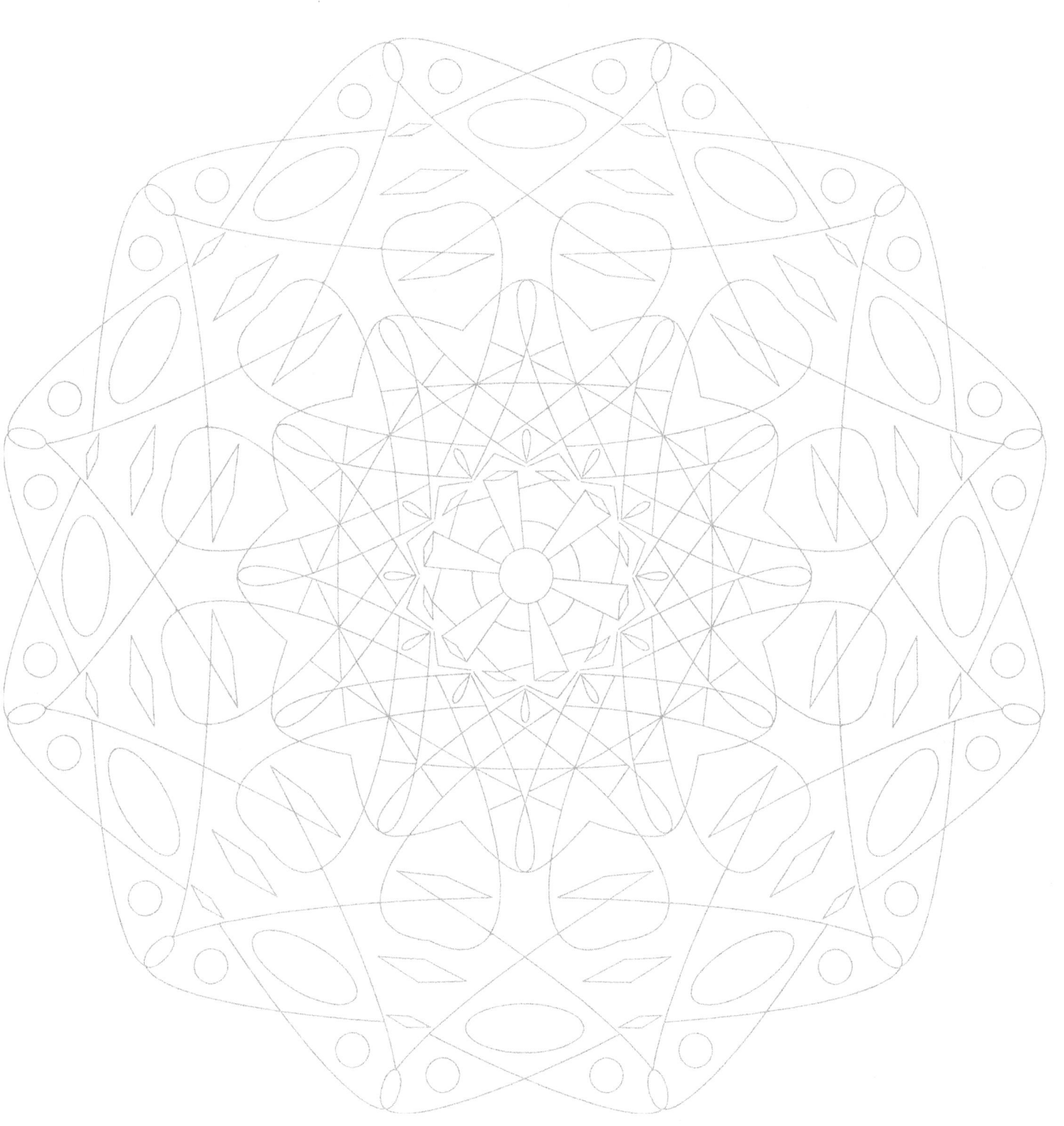

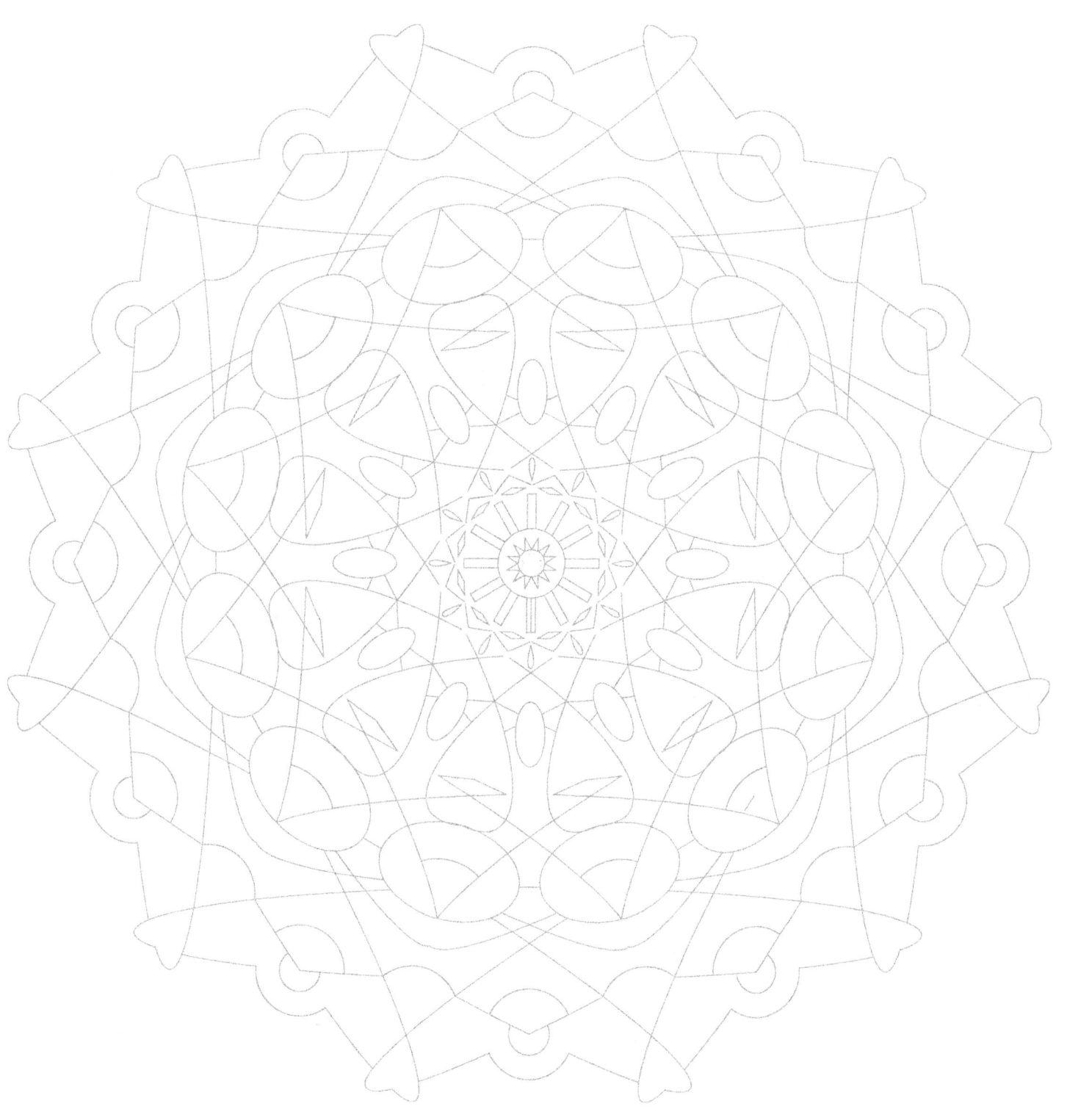

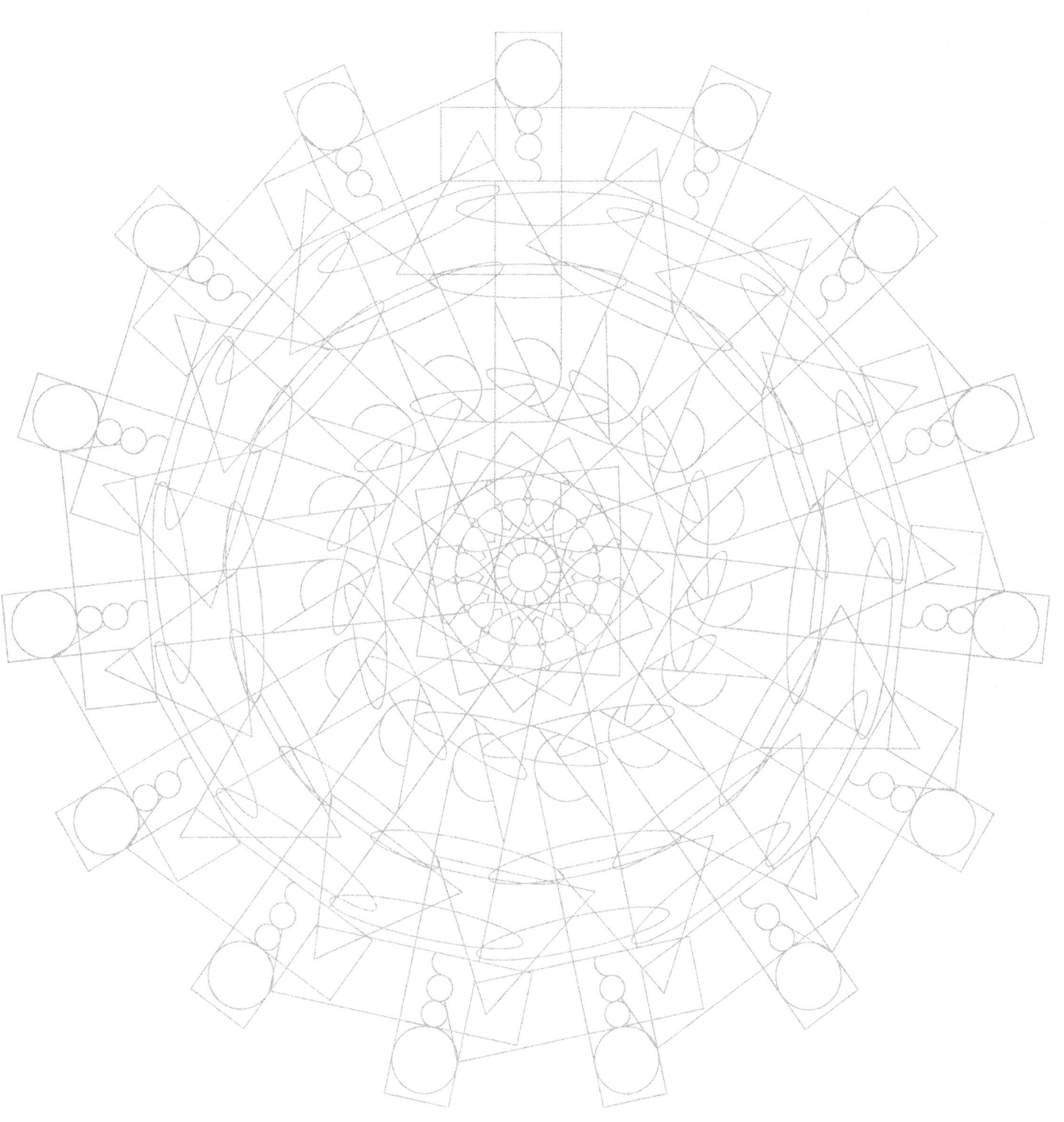

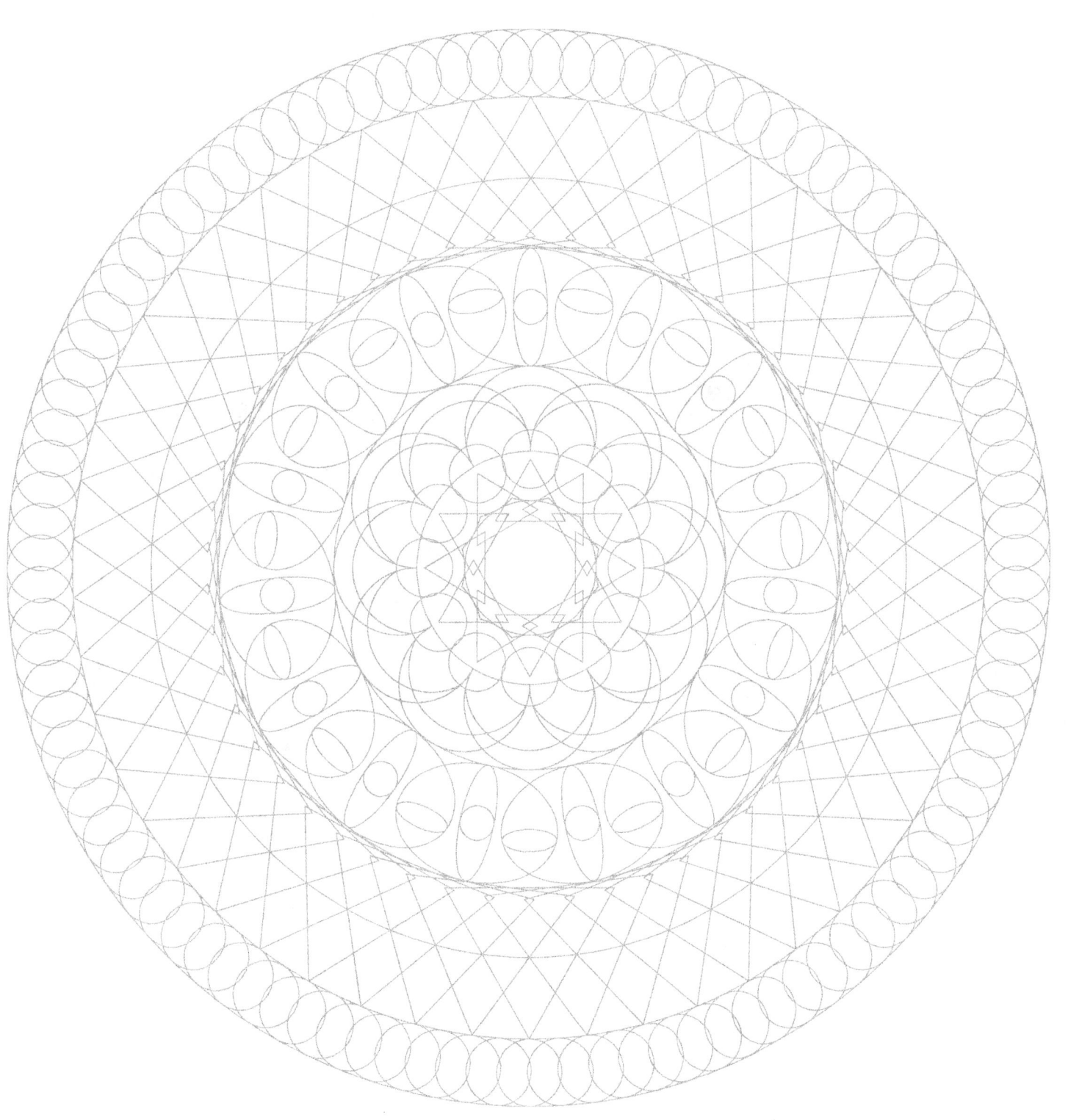

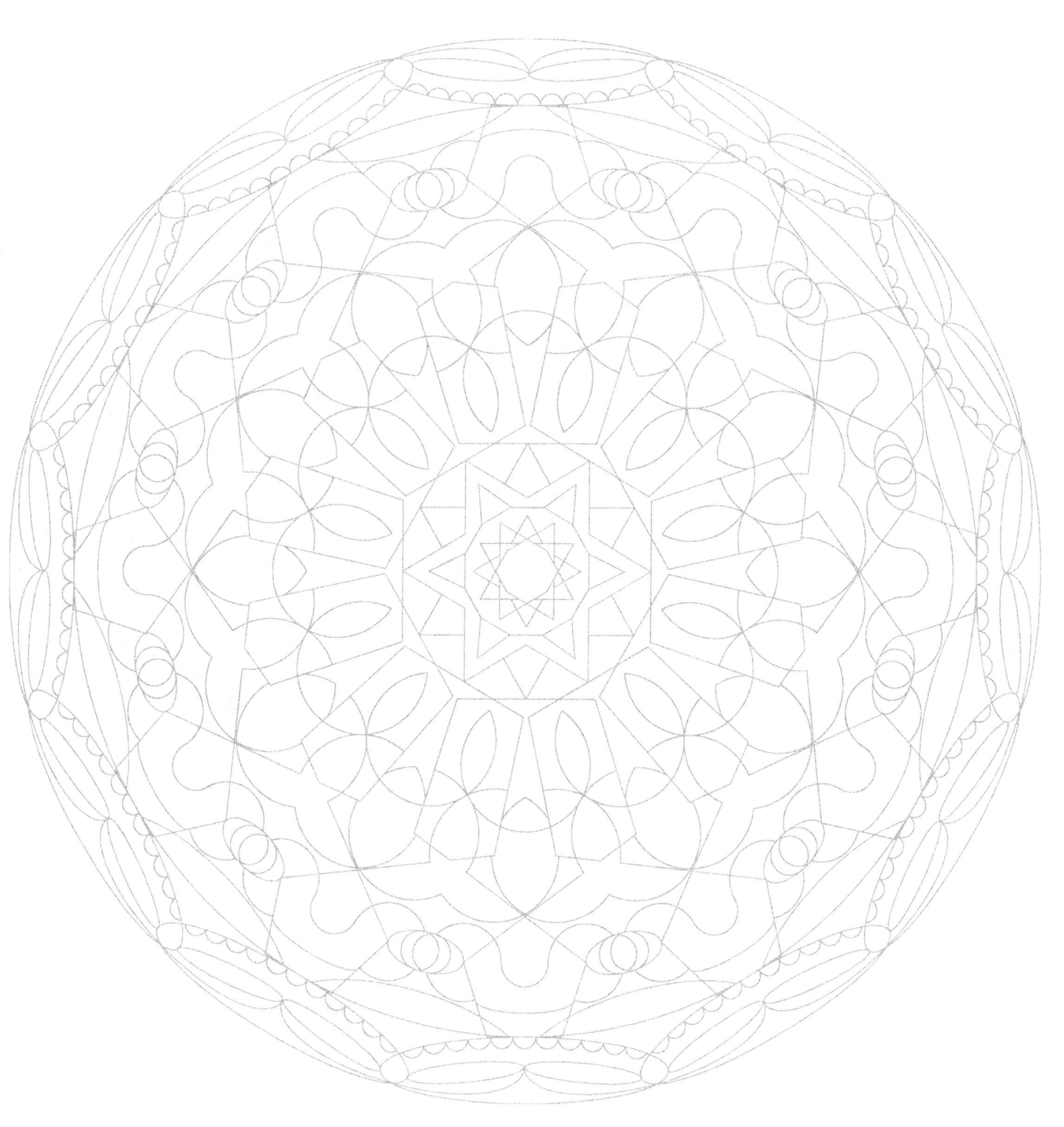

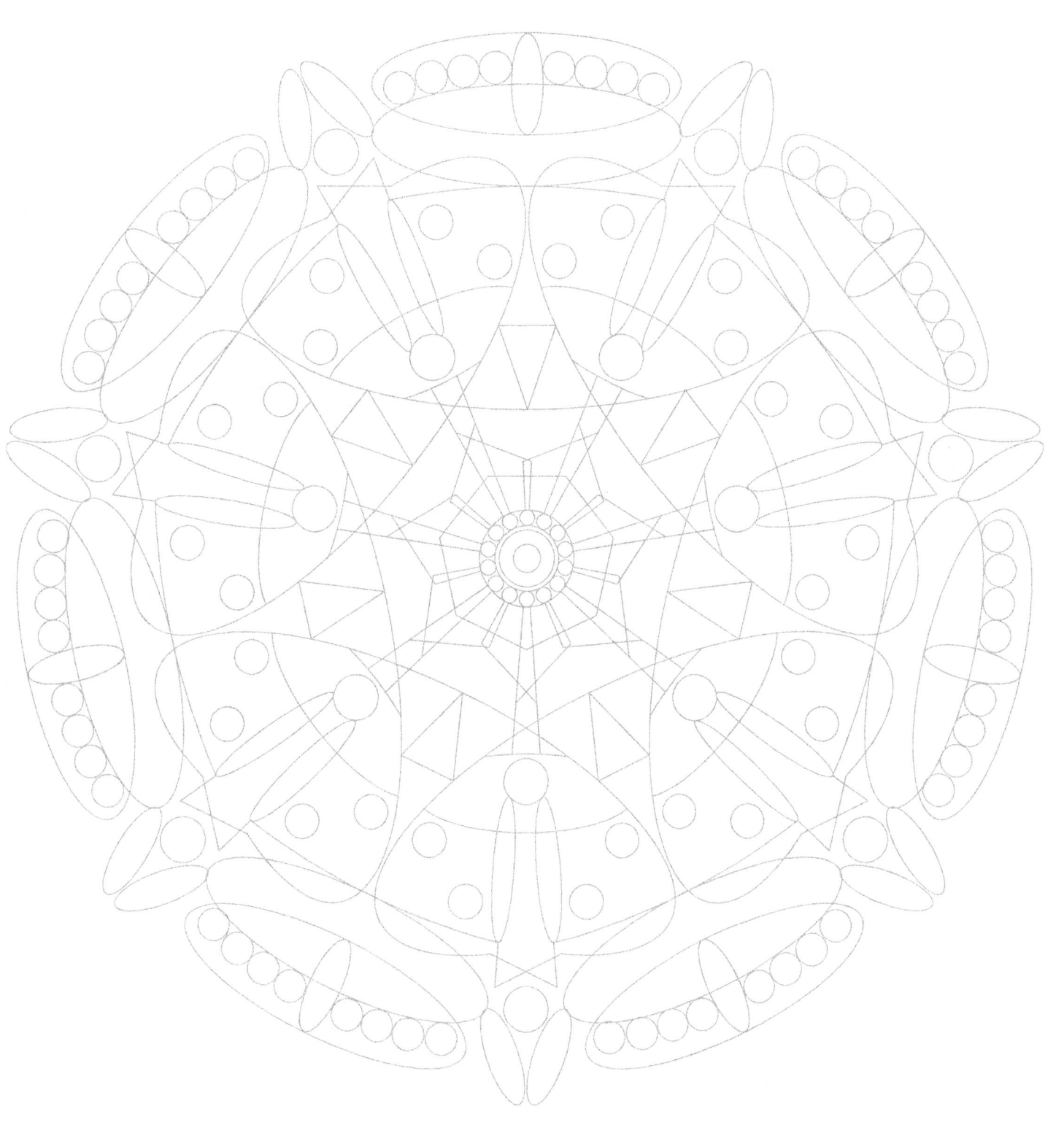

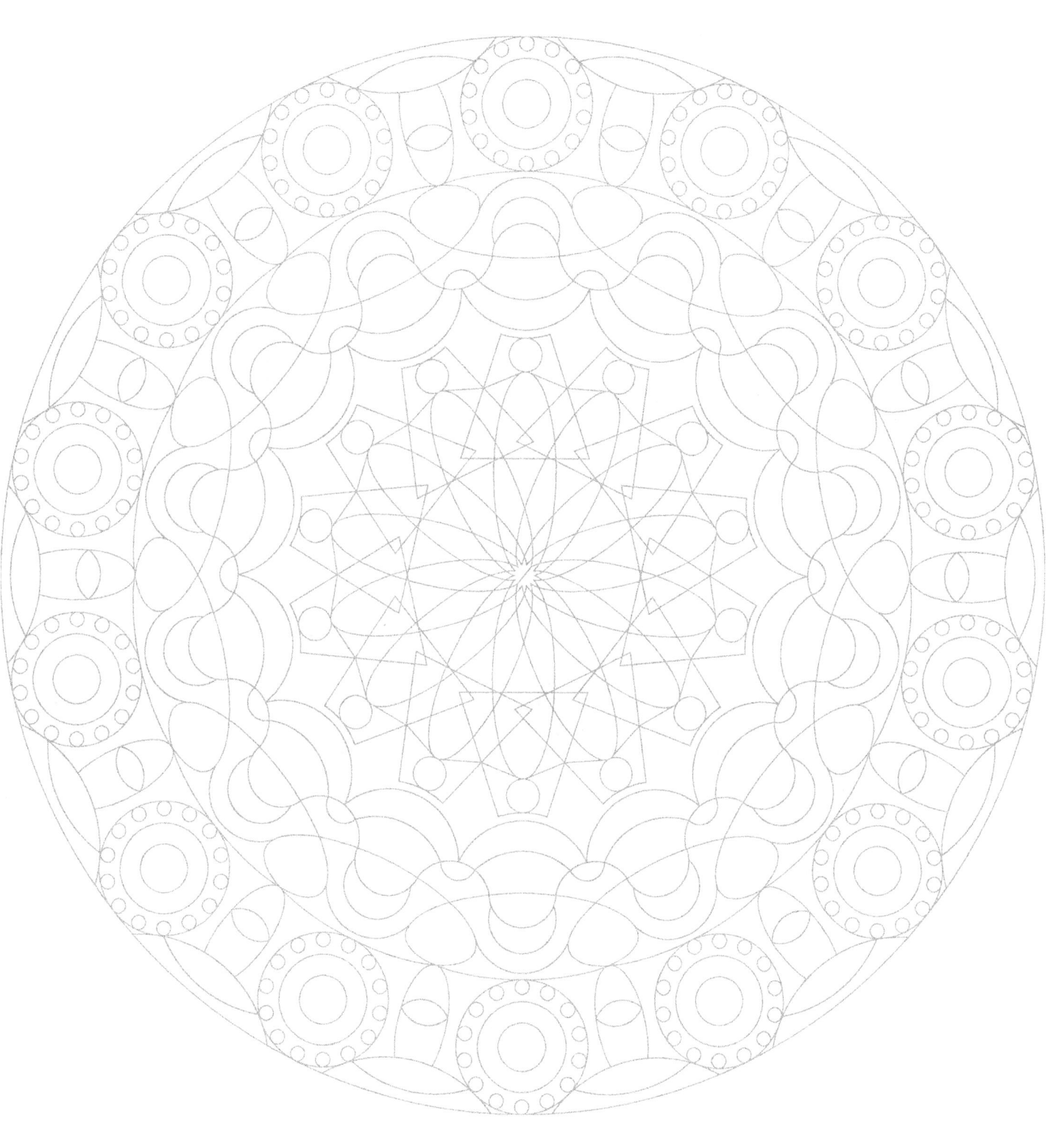

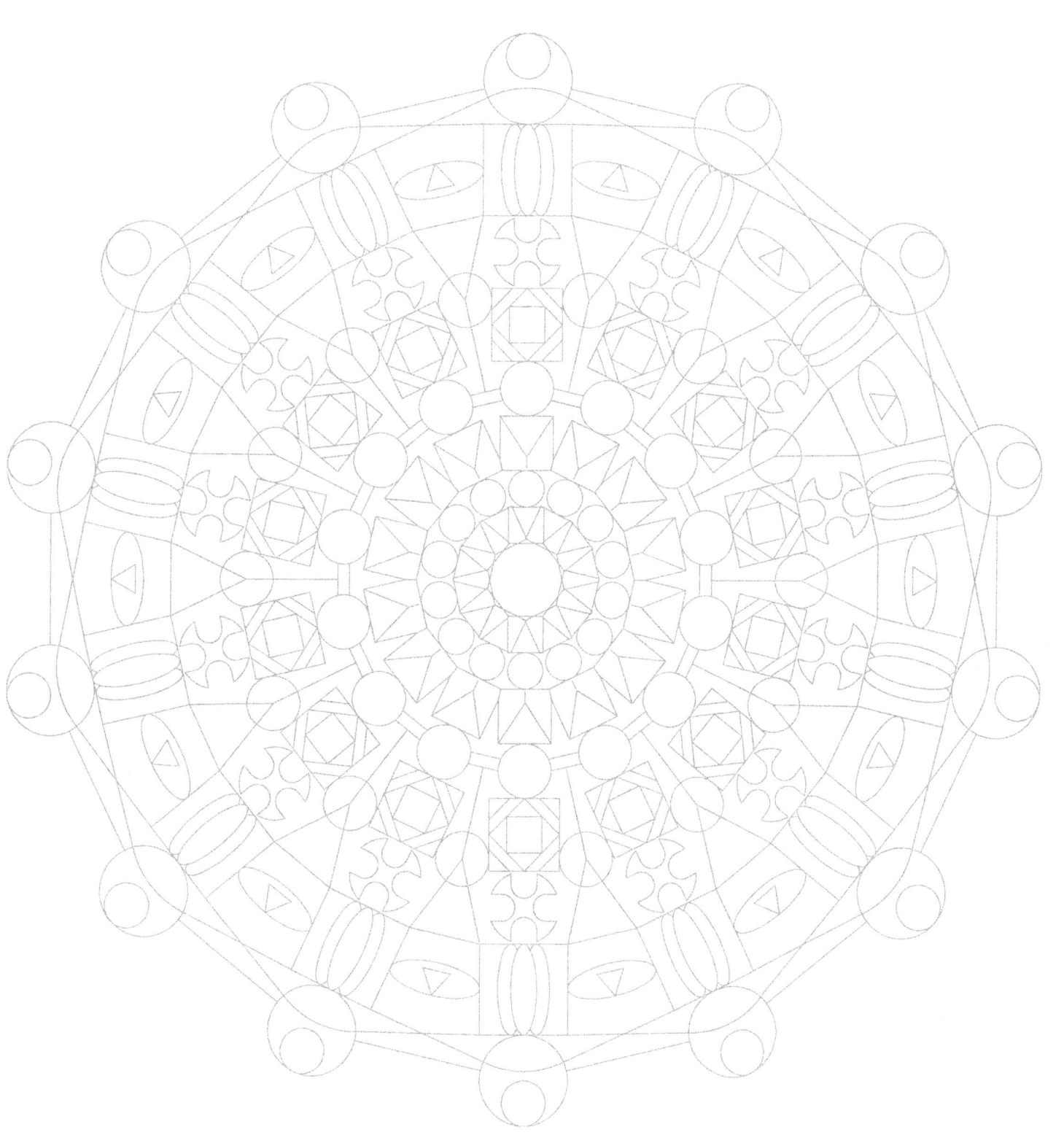

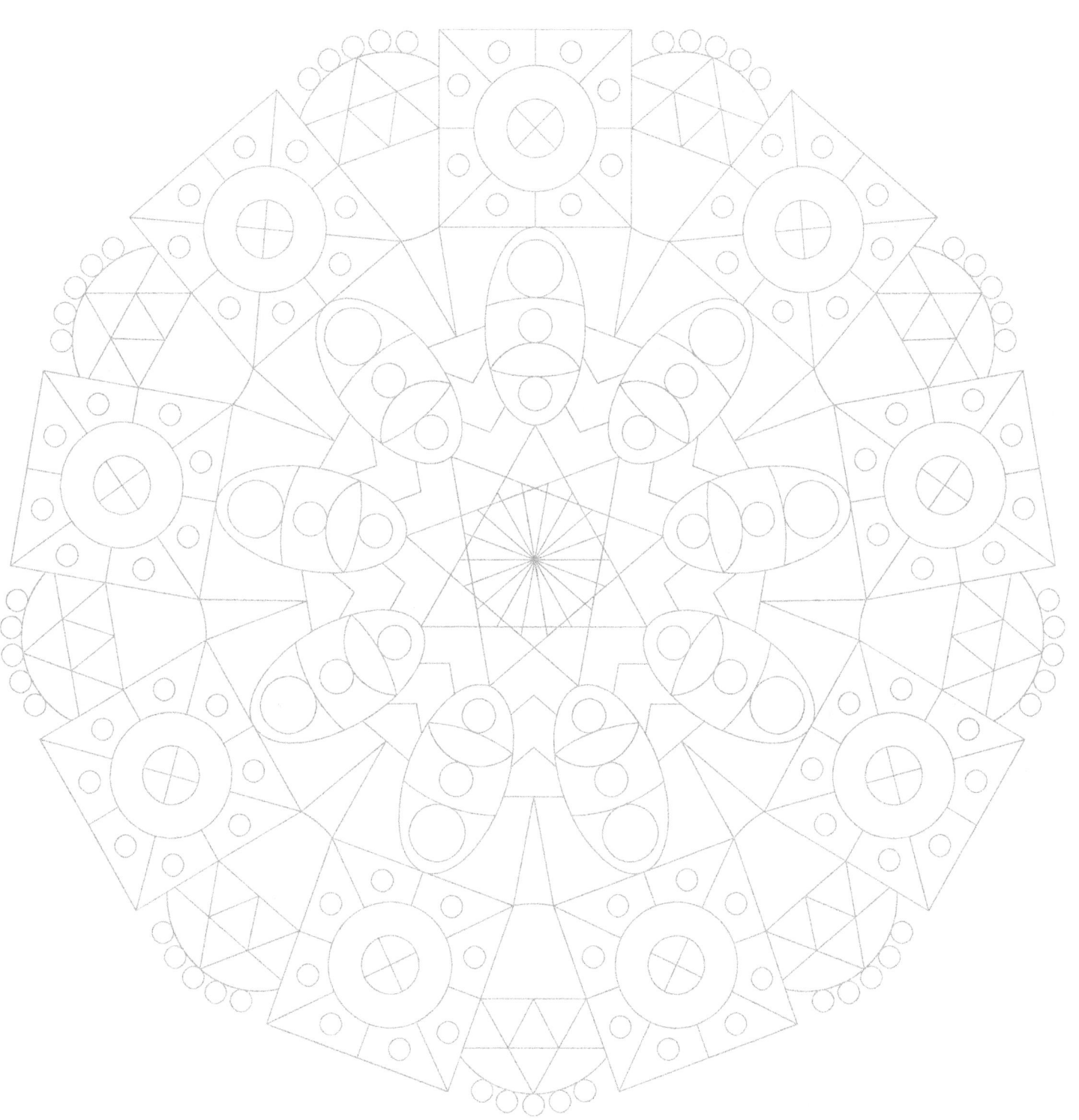

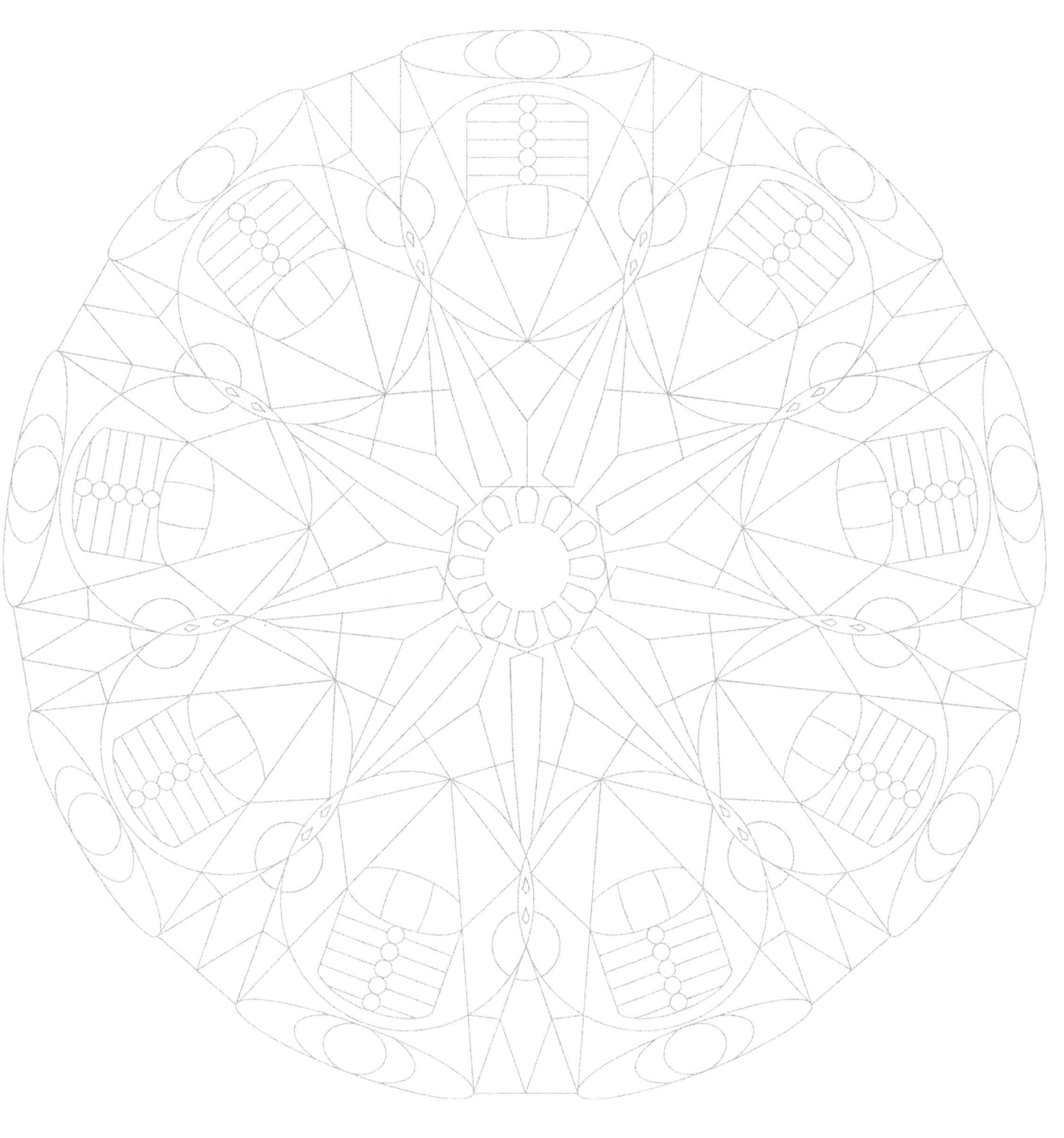

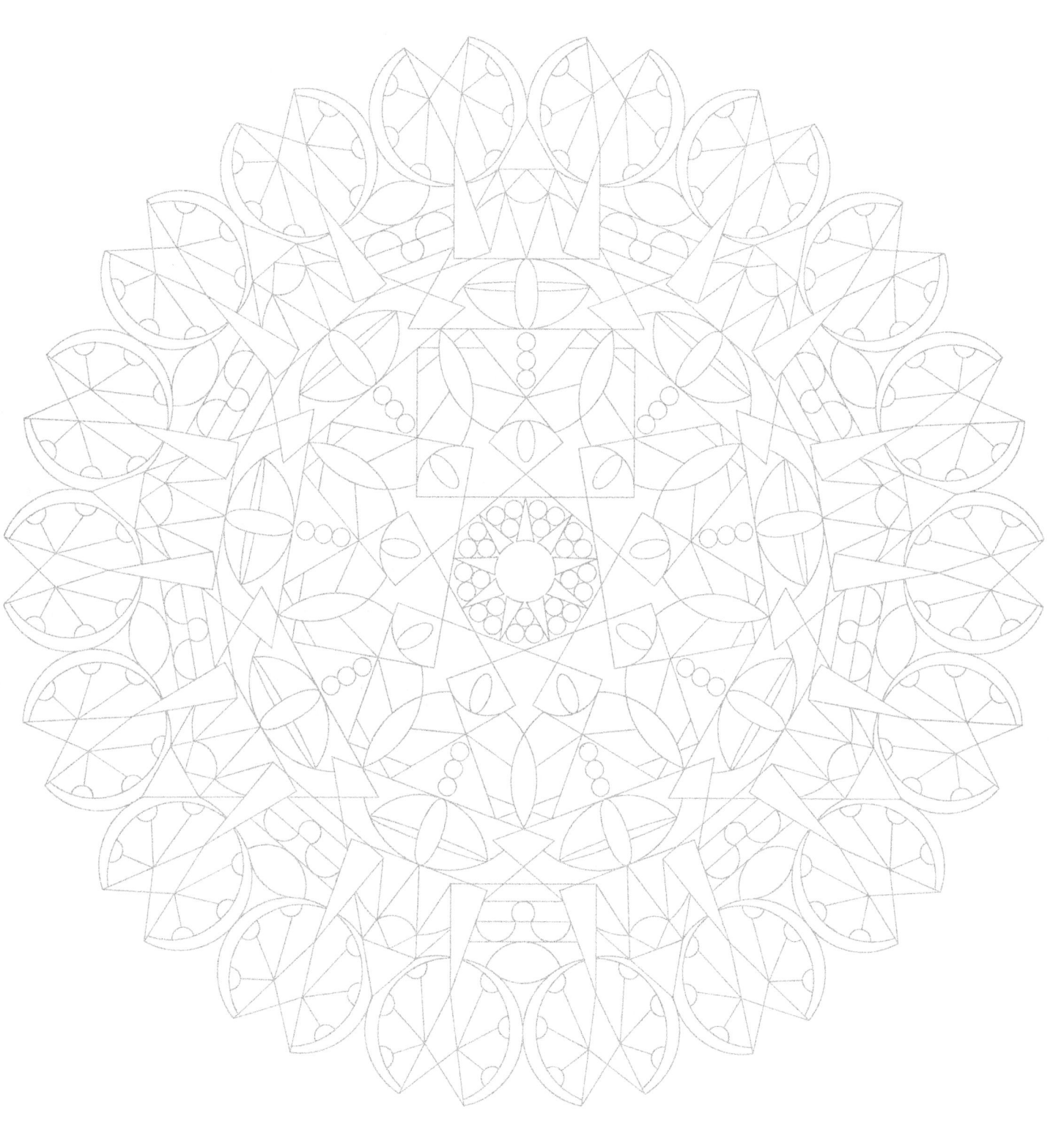

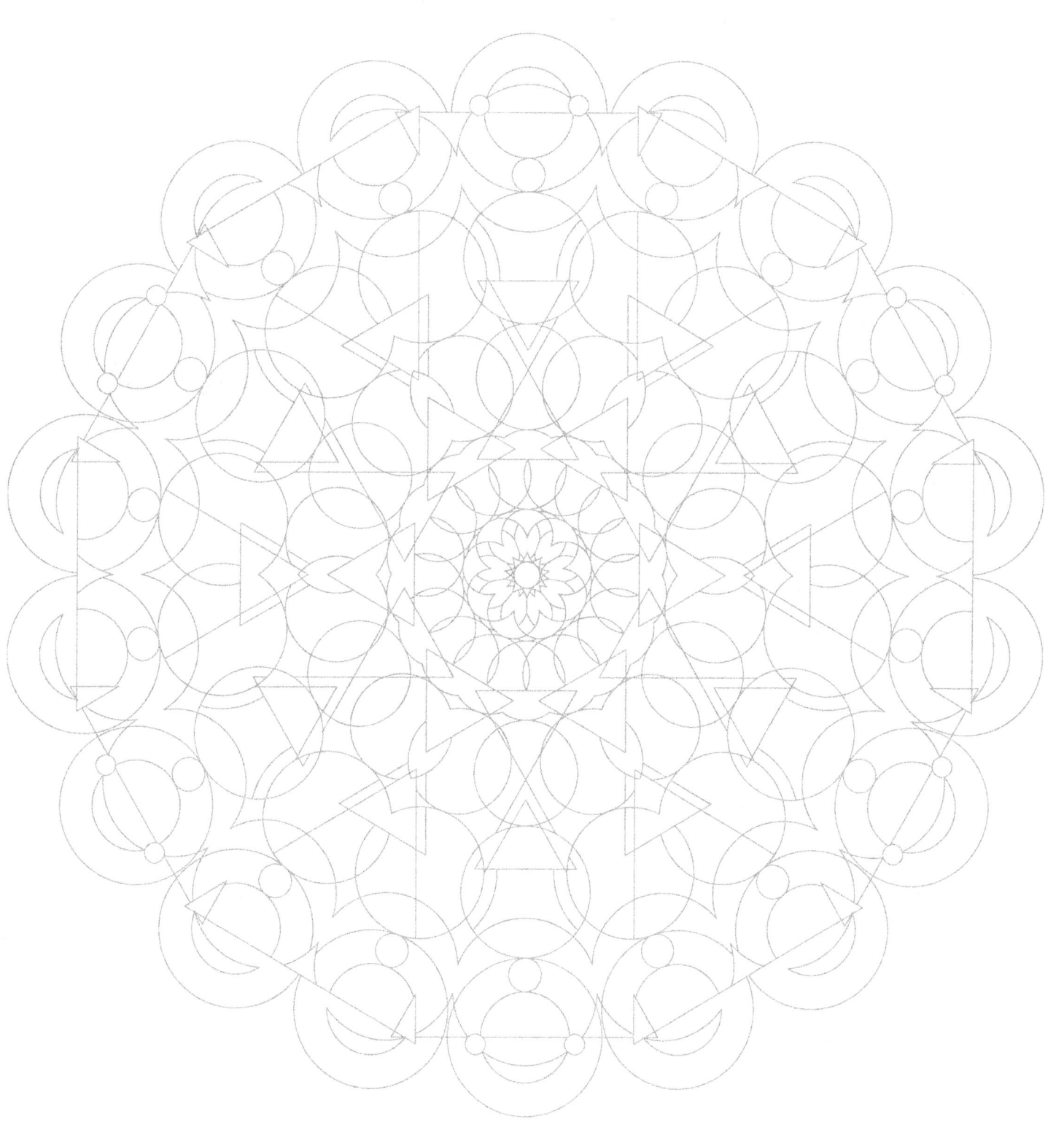

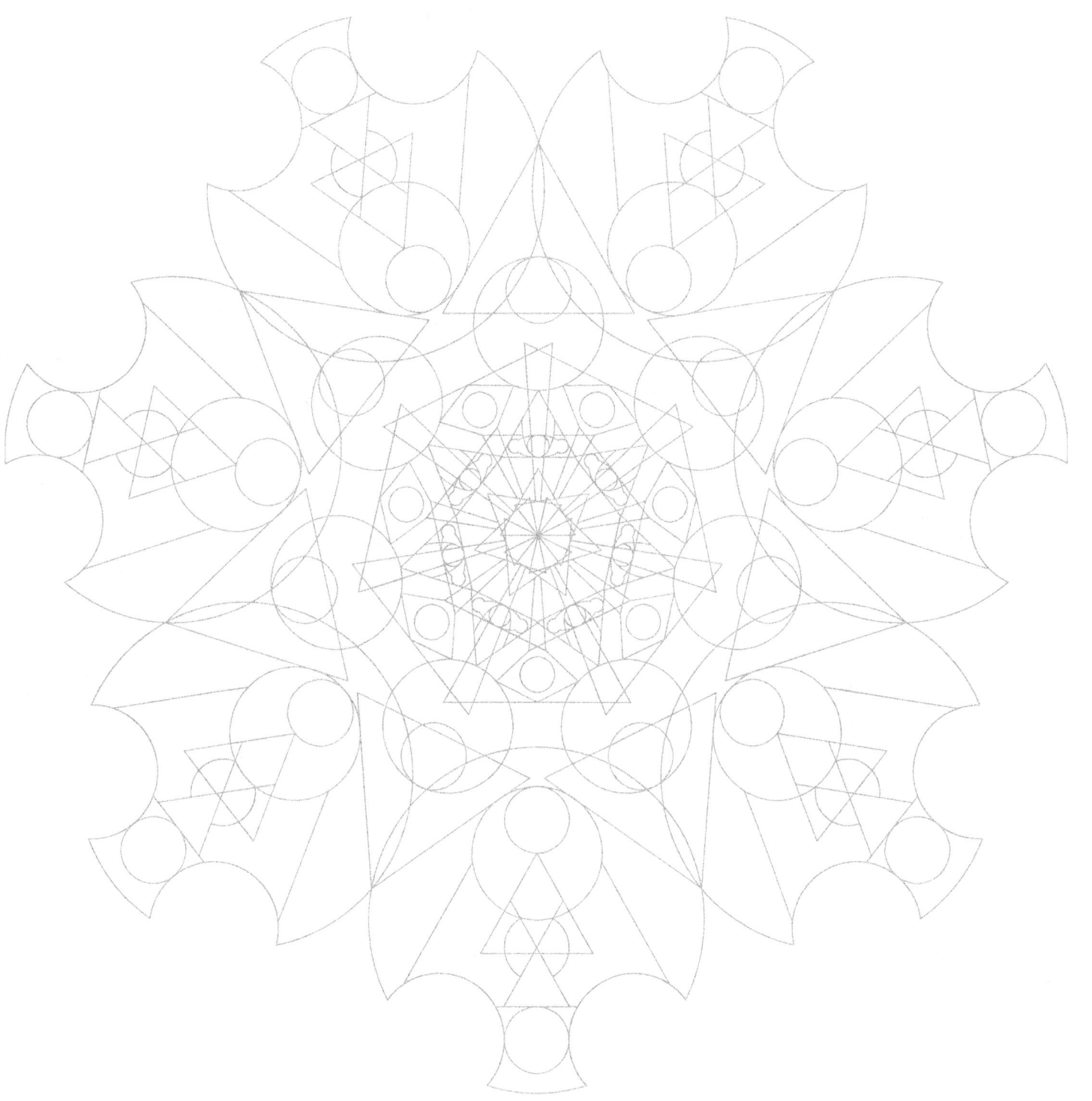

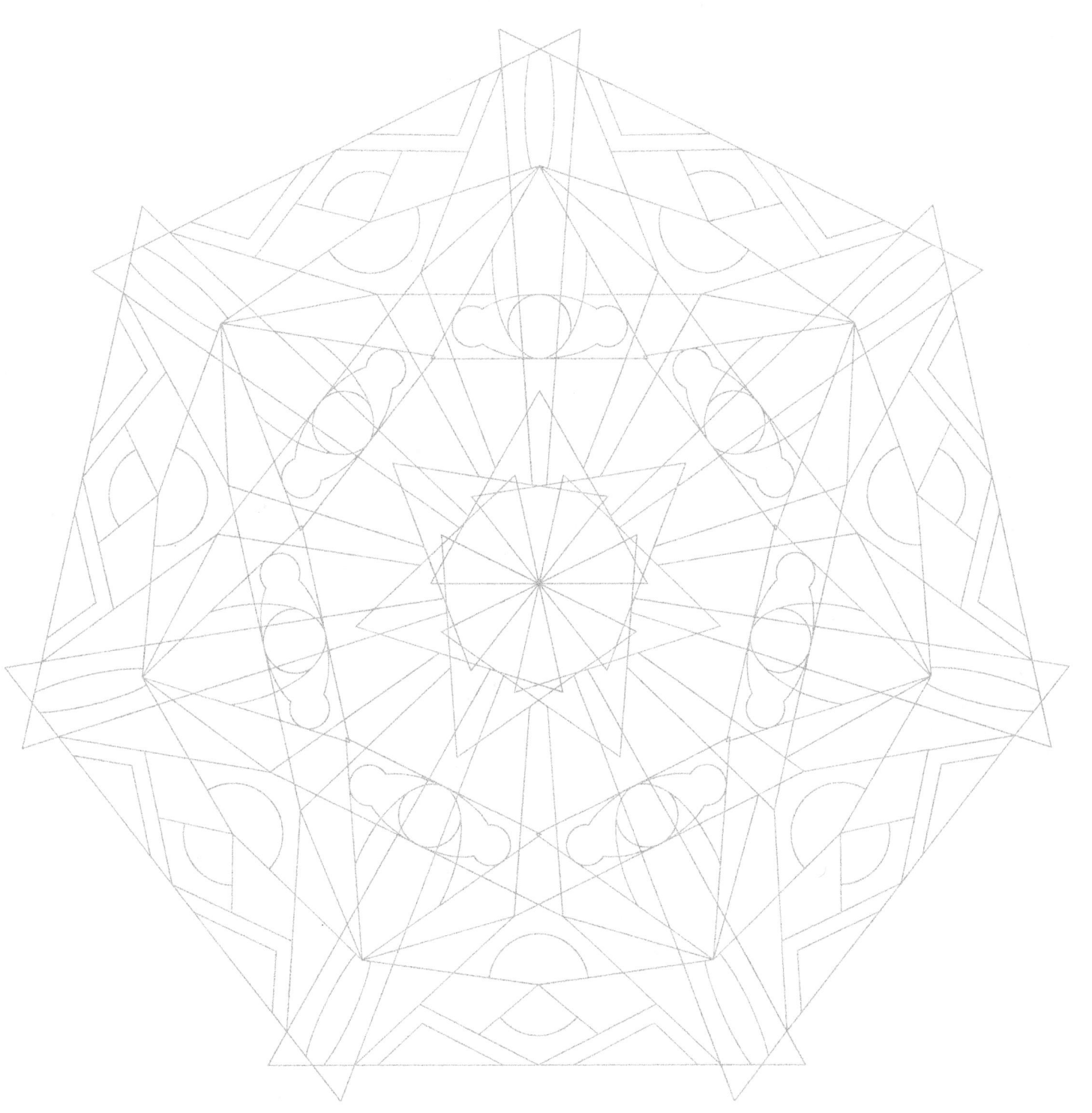

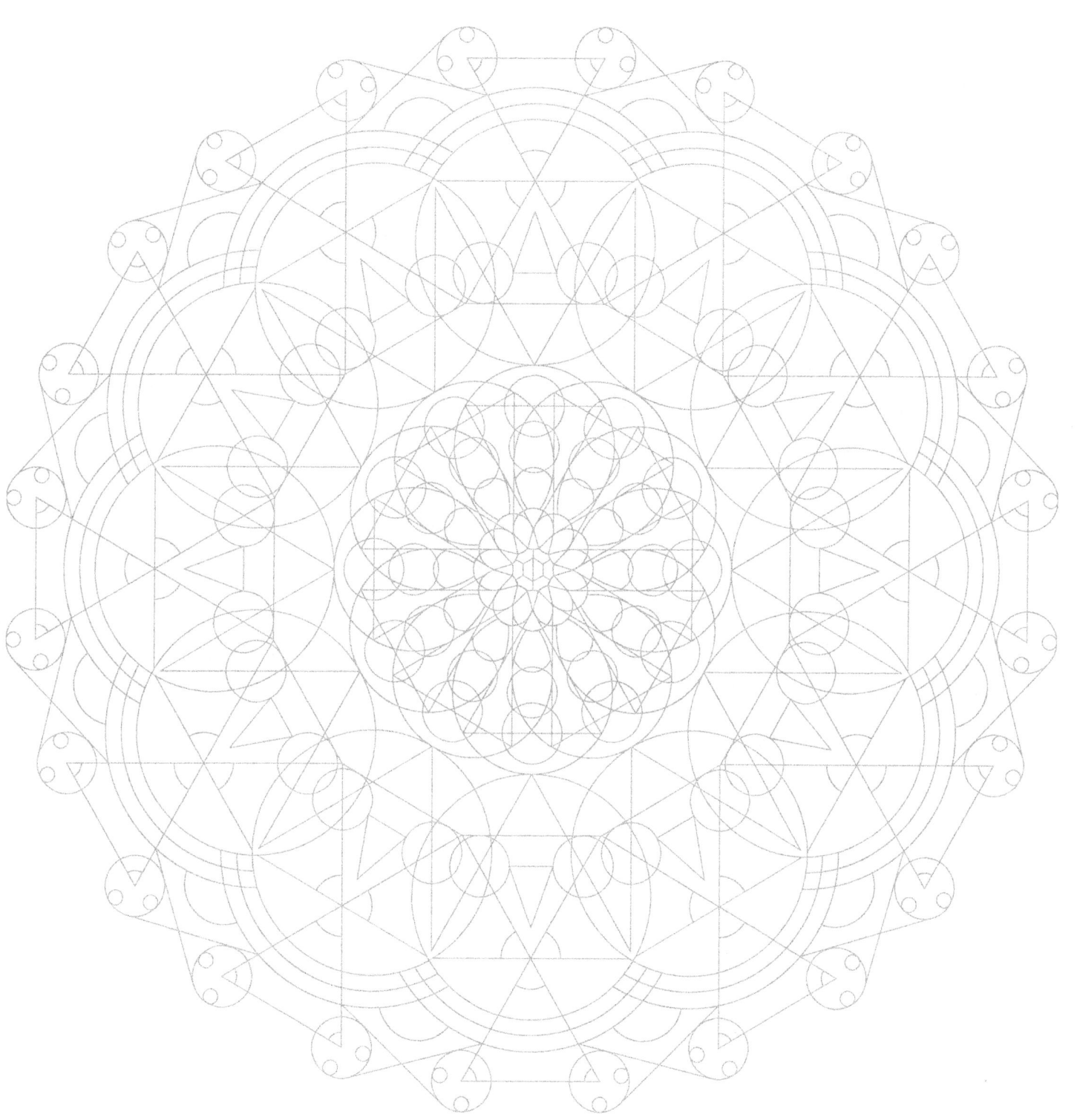

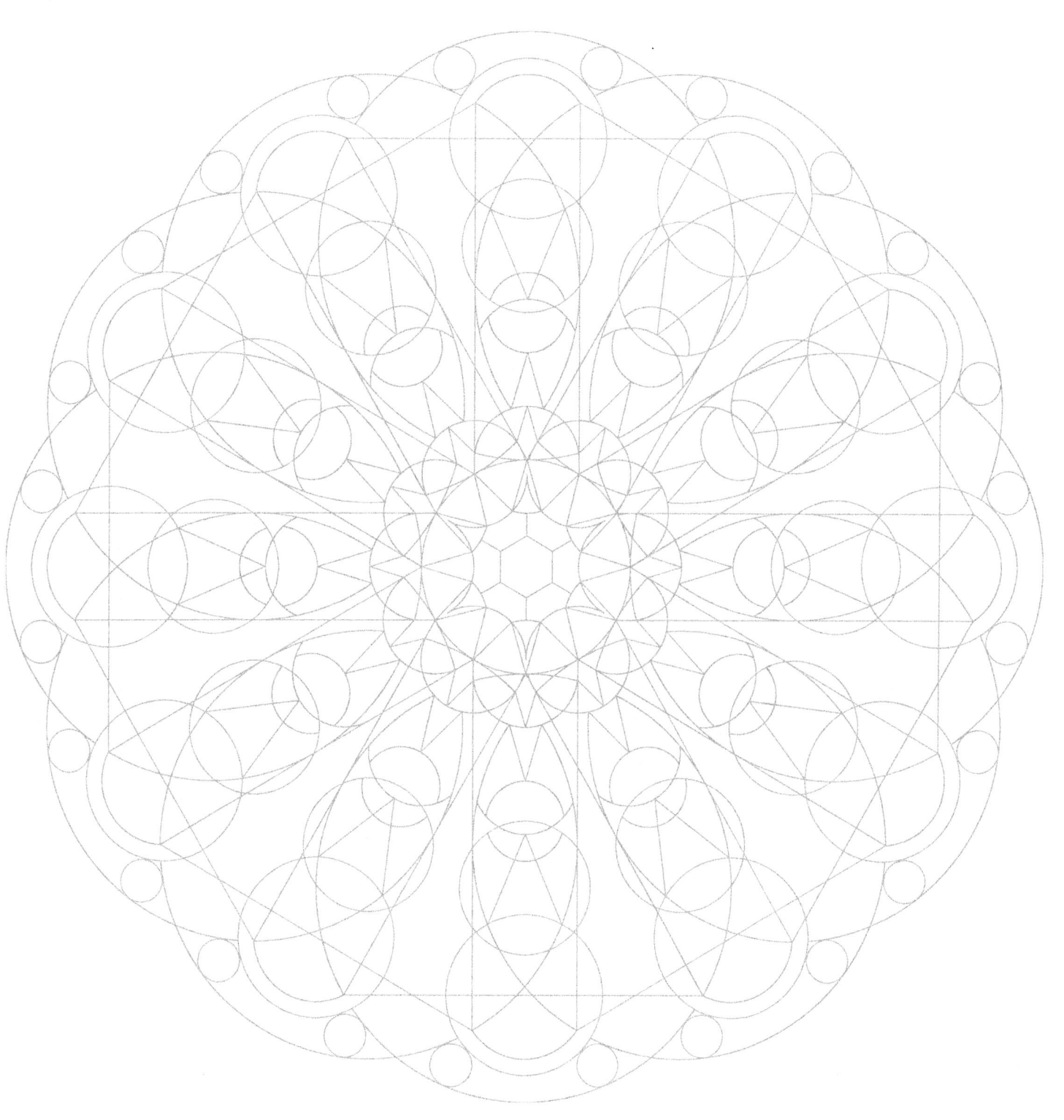

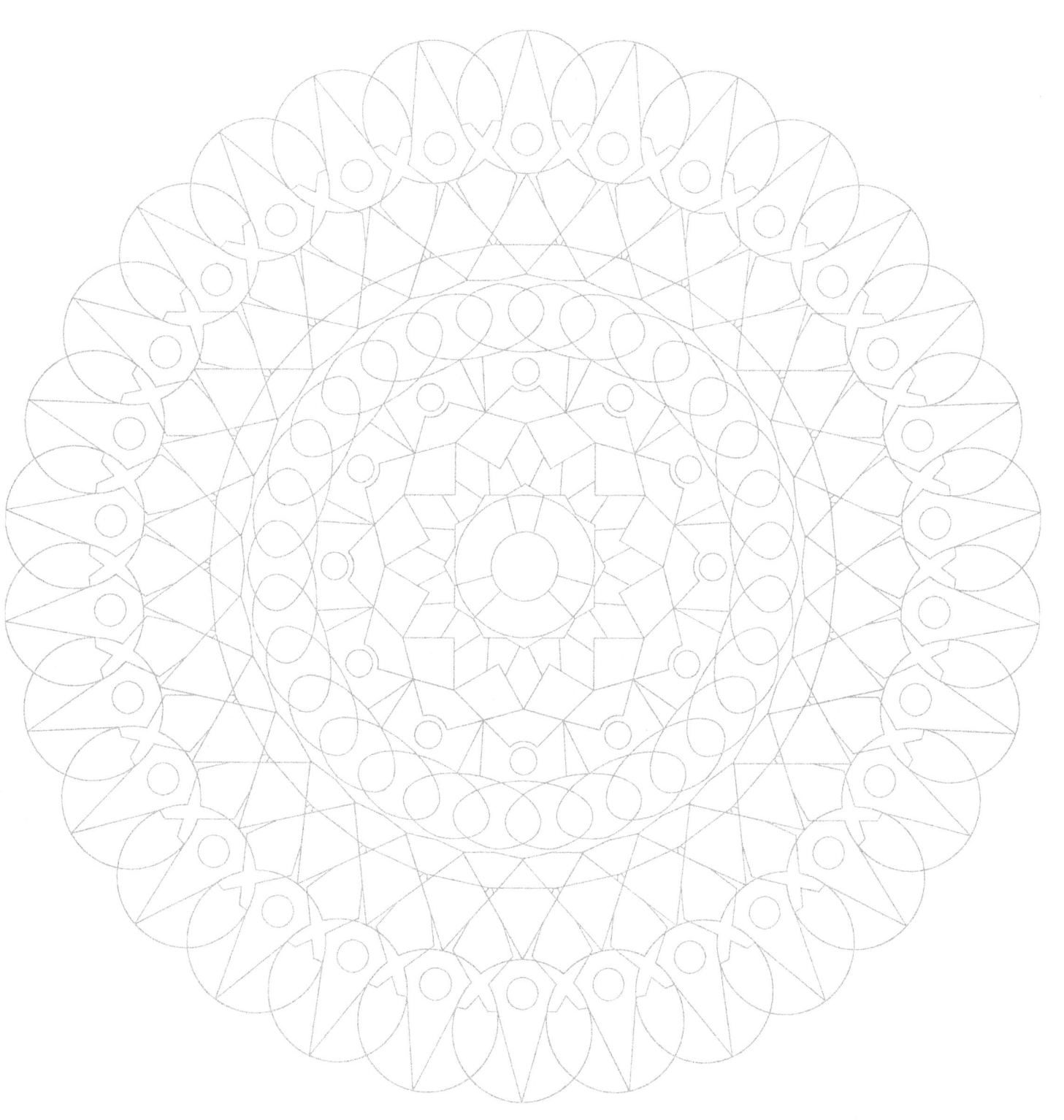

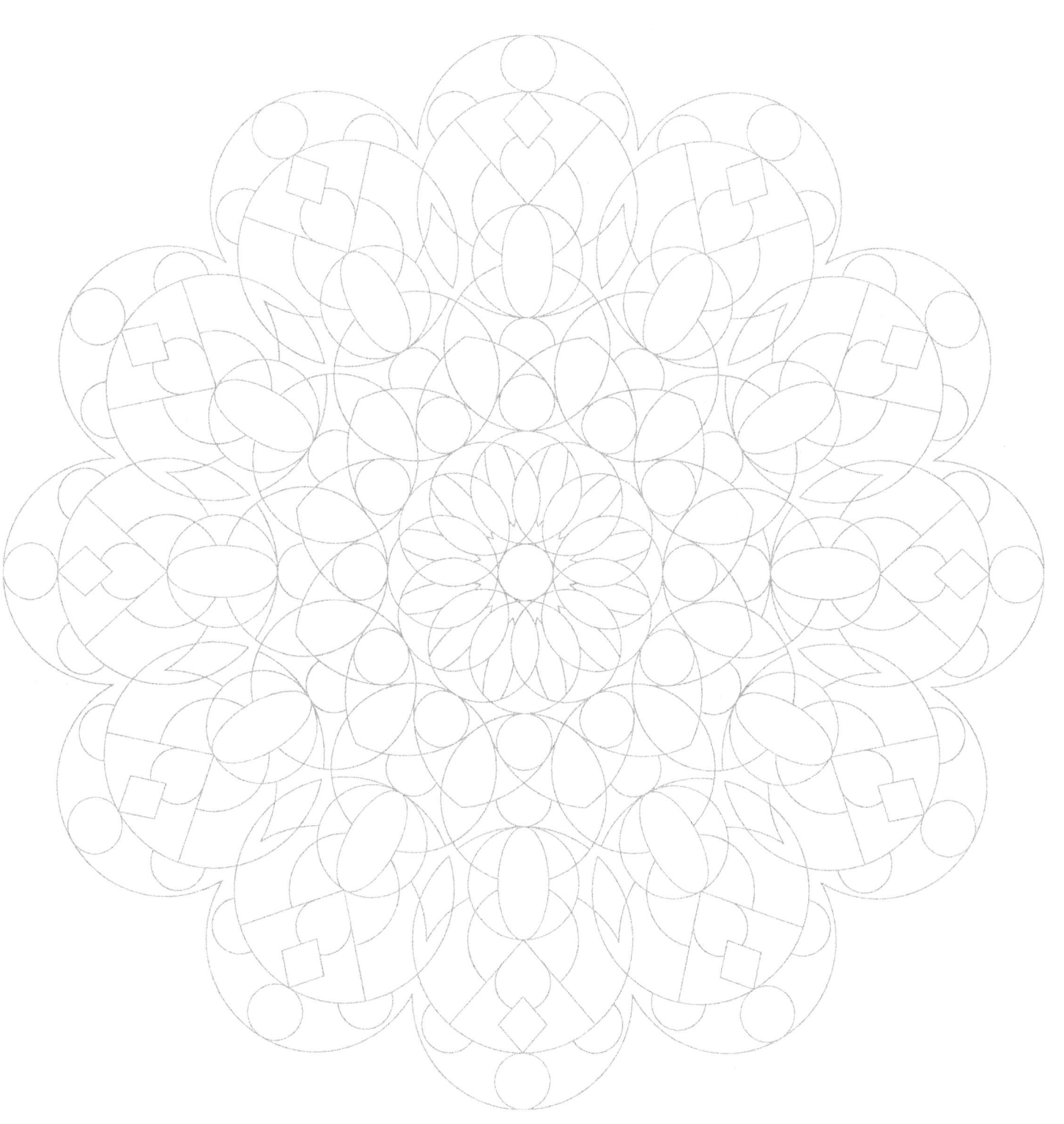

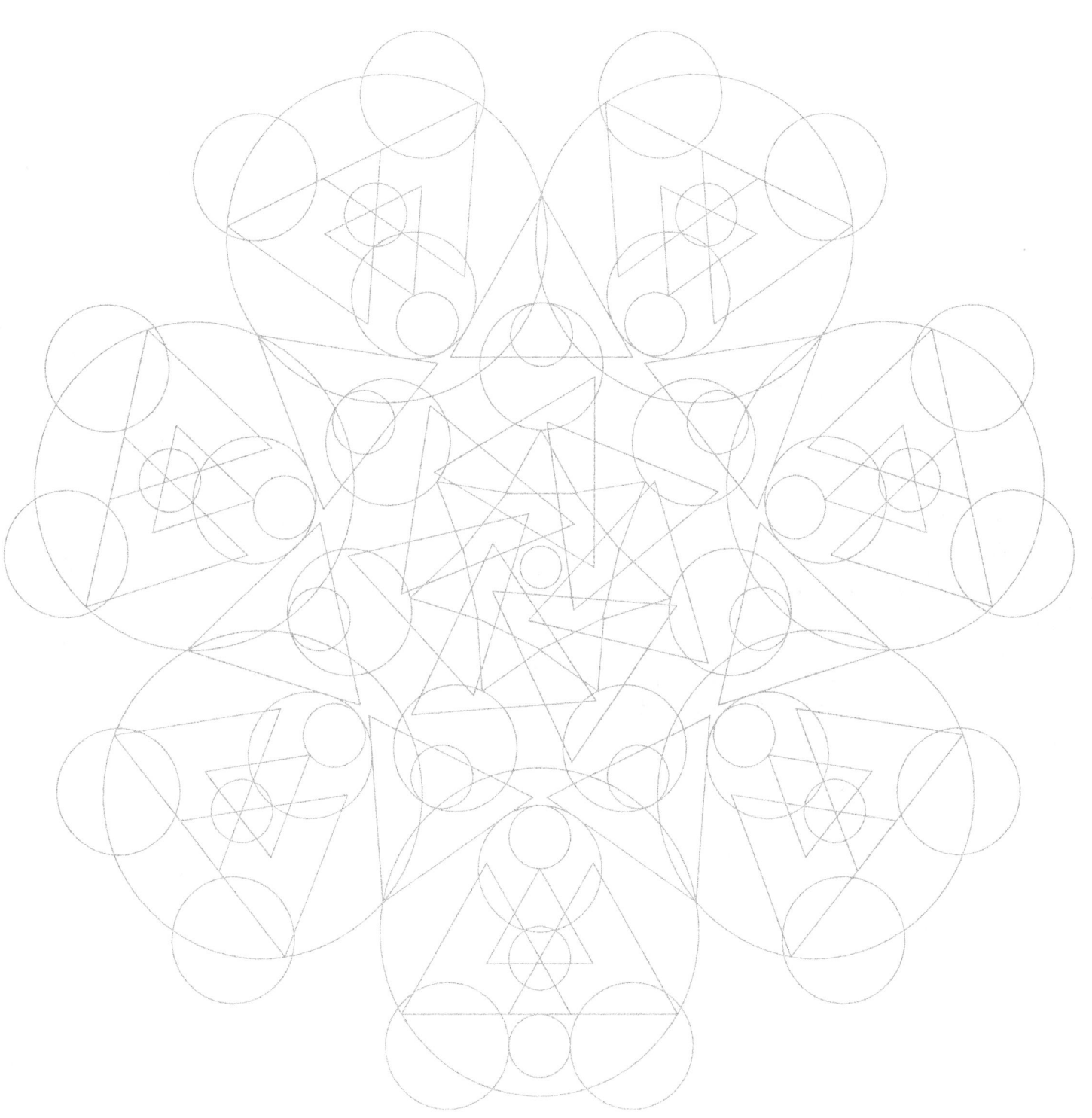

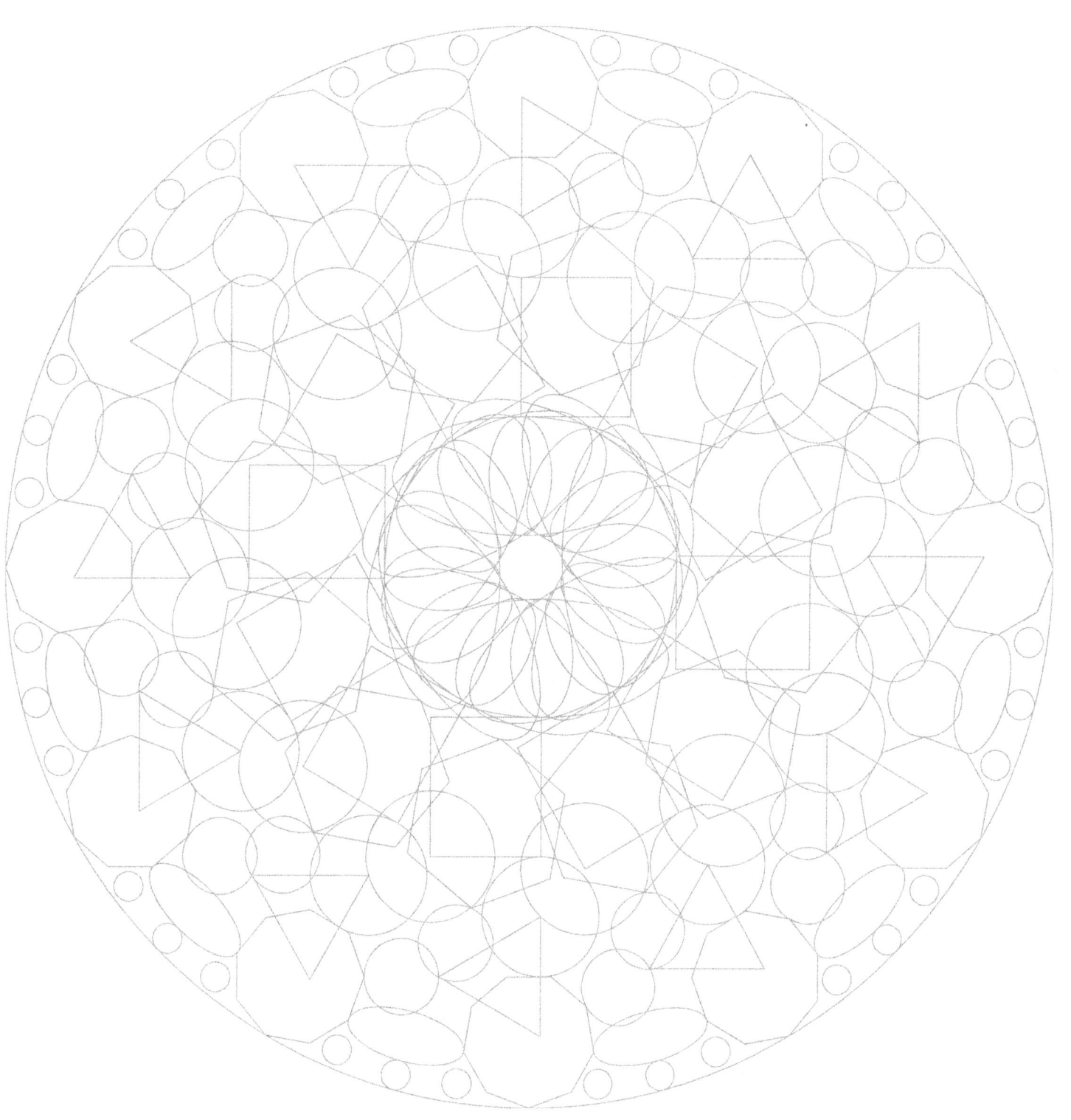

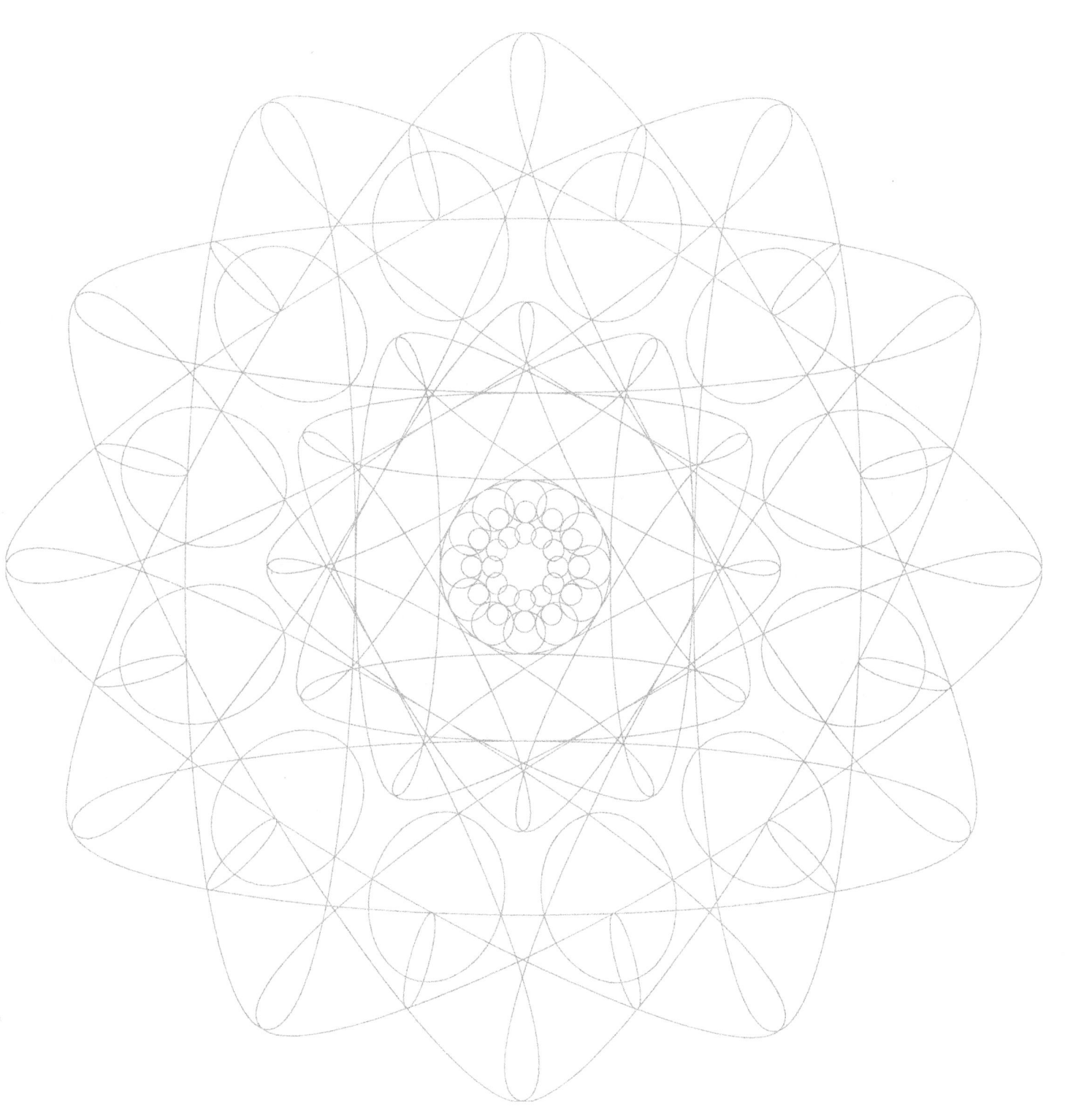

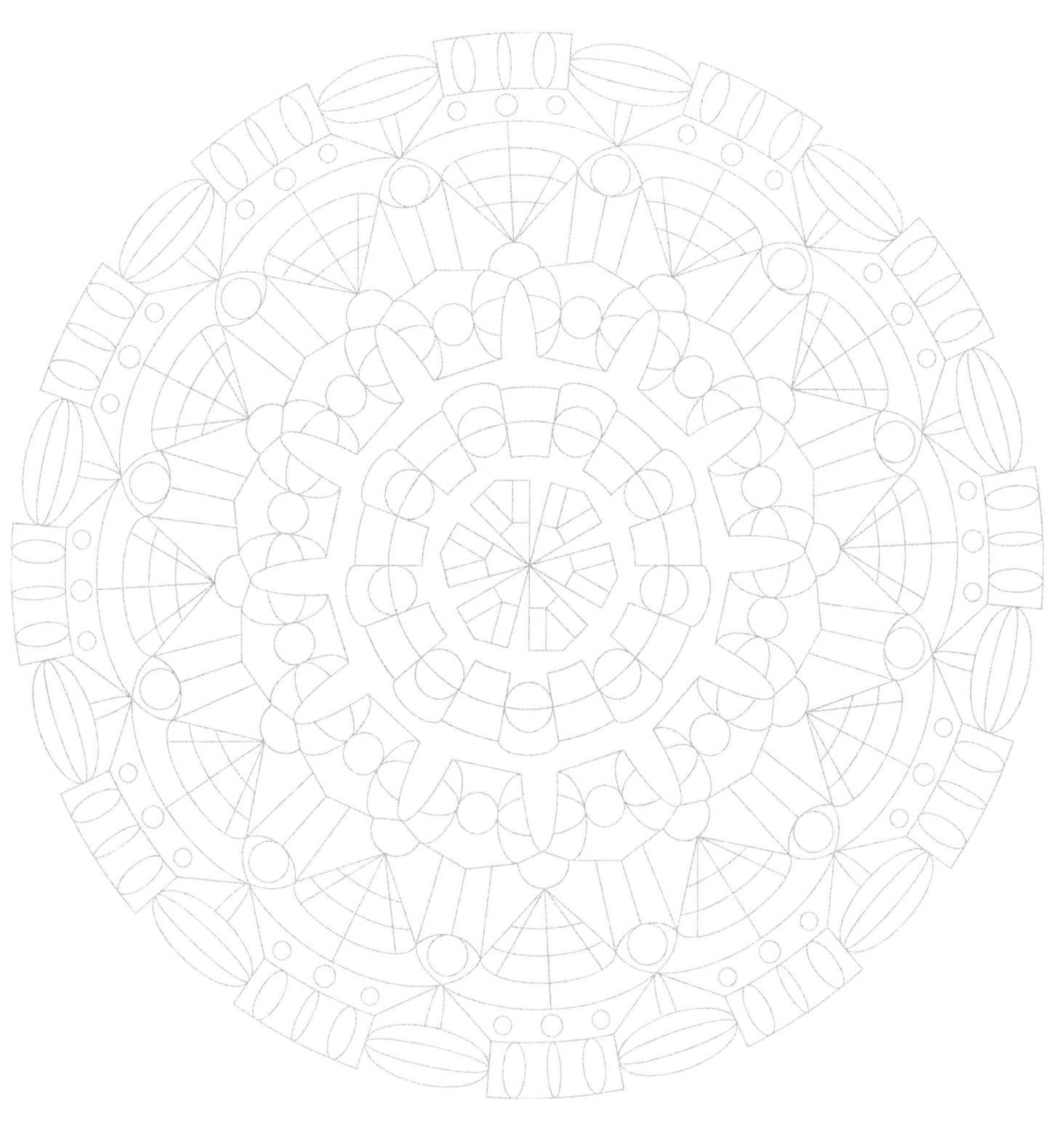